ADVANCE PRAISE FOR *THE INTEGRATION: A TRIUMPHANT JOURNEY OF TRIALS AND ERRORS*

This book offers an inspirational journey of the author's experience in pursuing her hopes and dreams. I It is far easier to follow the guidance of another to shape our journey forward, as there is truly no one size fits all. I appreciate her out of the box refractive thinking approach in offering wisdom and insights regarding her AH HA moments in life. Thank you for sharing to help ease our own journeys.

Dr. Cheryl Lentz, MS, DM
The Academic Entrepreneur
Founder of the 16 time award-winning series for doctoral scholars: The Refractive Thinker® www.RefractiveThinker.com

Dr. Swarna Shah's 5 A's solution that she details in 'The Integration' is an indispensable philosophy to apply to problems one might face at work, with the family, or anywhere else. The book was enjoyable to read and was one of those rare books that is entertaining and informative at the same time. It is always enlightening to read someone who talks about real problems and presents practical solutions as a parable of what we all face every day. The best part is when you take Swarna's approach to problem-solving and start using it for yourself. Make sure you give yourself the gift to move beyond your problems and create a life you love.

Tracy Repchuk
http://tracyrepchuk.com/
The White House Presidential Award Winner, 7 Time #1 International Bestselling Author including 31 Days to Millionaire Marketing Miracles

In this beautifully personal account, Dr Swarna Shah draws back the curtain on her life and takes you on an intimate journey through adversity, opportunity, and genuine kindness. Dr Shah exposes the art and power of positivity, as she shines a light on the enormous wealth to be gained from not only accepting our differences, but embracing them. Written with so much heart, it's impossible to resist the emotional spiral as you're carried up and down through the continuum of her life. On so many levels, Dr Shah's story is intensely relatable, making it relevant, uplifting, and completely authentic. A gentle yet poignant reminder of what can be achieved through basic human kindness and understanding, this book leaves you with rekindled faith in the human spirit and a deep-seated desire to live your best life.

Tina Cantrill RN, MBA, CPC
Burnout Prevention Guide and Sustainable Leadership Creator, 1st Degree Connectionist, Coaching & Leading Healthcare Professionals Through Burnout and Back To Life

I really enjoyed reading Dr. Shah's story. This is a heart-warming and encouraging read of a successful immigrant woman who has accomplished a great deal professionally, while instilling love, hard work and achievement as values in building a life for herself and her family.

Dr. Shah is a skilled and engaging storyteller. One story literally brought tears to my eyes. I enjoyed how she shared valuable life lessons while telling the story of her life. As a woman with young adult children, I could relate to the ever-changing dynamic between parents and children over the years. As they grow, we grow as well. We learn more about ourselves and how to adjust to fit the needs, strengths and personalities of each child. We learn how to let go and trust that what we taught them will carry them forward in life. All these things Dr. Shah weaves skillfully into a wonderful narrative, endearing you to herself and each of her family members.

I enjoyed reading about her personal and professional development, as a young wife, a working mother, and a leader. I found myself rooting for her during each stage of her life, as new interesting challenges arose. Even more compelling was Dr. Shah's perspective as an immigrant, sharing her love for family and ensuring that she and her husband instilled their Indian culture with their sons. It was very poignant to read about her first-person perspective on the value of our blended society, and the unique challenges that a family faces as they embrace American culture while maintaining their cultural identity.

Finally, I loved hearing her unique model 5 A's – that has helped her navigate life, and that she is now sharing with others. Take some time to read this book. You'll be glad you did, and you will also learn or be reminded of some things along the way.

Trina Ramsey
Executive Coach, Author, and Inspirational Speaker. Trina's debut book, Just Do You! A Declaration of Independence from Guilt, Obligation and Shame, became an Amazon Best Seller. Trina has also been nominated as Author of the Year: Personal Development in the Indie Author Legacy Awards. Learn more about Trina's work at justdoyouinstitute.com.

In *The Integration*, Dr. Swarna Shah powerfully shares her life experiences. Her sharing helps encourage and equip men and women to move forward in a positive way...No matter where they are in life. Dr. Swarna shares a key insight that happiness is only possible when we are operating with joy on all cylinders. In this dynamic book, she shows us how to achieve happiness!

Rebecca Hall Gruyter
Empowerment Leader & Influencer Expert

I was excited when I received the advanced manuscript of this book. I know that Dr. Swarna Shah's life has been filled with many milestones in both her personal and professional life.

The author's desire to reach out and help women find a balance in their lives so that they can have a fulfilling professional and personal life is commendable.

It was enlightening to follow how an immigrant from India to the United States forged her medical career while having a wonderful marriage and raising three sons. Accomplishing all these tasks is not easy for anyone. Swarna has combined the elements of her history and put it together with incidents that happened to others to illustrate the complexities of life in a poignant and entertaining fashion. In essence, her story becomes a parable to all women of a healthy way to approach life and that it is possible to reach all your desires.

What is made clear is that the process is not always easy and that obstacles constantly crop up whether they involve you or those you are close to at work or in your family. Her story is very realistic as it constantly shows the everyday problems we all face, and then how to overcome them. It doesn't take superhuman qualities to do so. Instead, Swarna shows that common sense, wisdom, and a mindful approach to things is what will help us to overcome life's issues.

I am excited to see the next steps she takes in her life as she moves forward to help others in this new way. As a gifted doctor, Dr. Swarna has helped many through her medical expertise. I am confident that she will use her talents through this book and others, as well as personal interaction, to help many women achieve a wonderful balance in life.

Nicole Dauphinee Thessen
News Anchor, Reporter, #1 Bestselling Author

When I finished reading "The Integration: A Triumphant Journey of Trials and Errors," I had to start it again. It was so full of so many practical tips on how to achieve better balance in one's professional and personal life that I wanted to make sure that I didn't miss anything! Dr. Swarna Shah does a superb job of sharing her experiences with the reader and showing how so much of what she went through is relatable to most working women. Instead of fighting our circumstances, as some of us do, Swarna embraces them and shows us how to do that too. I feel she is aligned with my mission to empower women to level up without burning out or opting out so that they can live their best lives in their homes, work and communities."

Susan Treadgold
Certified High Performance Coach, Transformational Trainer and Best Selling Author of The High Performing Woman: 52 Take Action Tips for Greater Confidence, Energy and Impact

THE INTEGRATION

A TRIUMPHANT JOURNEY OF TRIALS AND ERRORS

THE INTEGRATION

A TRIUMPHANT JOURNEY OF TRIALS AND ERRORS

SWARNA B. SHAH M.D.

THE DP GROUP LLC

Copyright and Disclaimer

We support copyright of all intellectual property. Copyright protection continues to spark the seed of creativity in content producers, ensures that everyone has their voice heard through the power of words and the captivity of a story. Uniqueness of culture and content has been passed down through generations of writing and is the DNA of every intelligent species on our planet. This publication is intended to provide helpful and informative material. It is not intended to diagnose, treat, cure, or prevent any health problem or condition, nor is intended to replace the advice of a physician. No action should be taken solely on the contents of this book. Always consult your physician or qualified health-care professional on any matters regarding your health and before adopting any suggestions in this book or drawing inferences from it.

The author and publisher specifically disclaim all responsibility for any liability, loss or risk, personal or otherwise, which is incurred as a consequence, directly or indirectly, from the use or application of any contents of this book. Any and all product names referenced within this book are the trademark of their respective owners. None of these owners have sponsored, authorized, endorsed, or approved this book. Always read all information provided by the manufacturers' product labels before using their products. The author and publisher are not responsible for claims made by manufacturers.

Copyright © 2018 by The DP Group, LLC

ISBN-13 978-1-949513-00-4

All rights reserved. No part of this publication may be reproduced, distributed, or transmitted in any form or by any means, including photocopying, recording, or other electronic or mechanical methods, without the prior written permission of the publisher, except in the case of brief quotations embodied in critical reviews and certain other noncommercial uses permitted by copyright law. For permission requests, see the back of the book for details.

Ordering Information:

Quantity Sales: Special discounts are available on quantity purchases by corporations, associations, and others. For details, contact the publisher at contact@divyaparekh.com

Printed in the United States of America

First Edition

ACKNOWLEDGMENTS

Divya Parekh's coaching was the portal to getting my book published and becoming a #1 International Bestseller!

Divya worked her magic on me as she teased memories out of me that I hadn't thought about in a long time. Furthermore, she helped me connect those memories to talents and craft a message to help others. Divya helped me create a framework for my multi-layered book. As my cheerleader, her encouragement, knowledge, and partnership gave me a complete blueprint for the whole writing, publishing and marketing process.

DEDICATION

I dedicate this book to my family and friends who have been a constant source of encouragement and inspiration. I couldn't be who I am without all of you in my life.

FOREWORD

I was excited when I received the advanced manuscript of this book. I know that Dr. Swarna Shah's life has been filled with many milestones in both her personal and professional life. The author's desire to reach out and help women find a balance in their lives so that they can have a fulfilling professional and personal life is commendable.

It was enlightening to follow how an immigrant from India to the United States forged her medical career while having a wonderful marriage and raising three sons. Accomplishing all these tasks is not easy for anyone. Swarna has combined the elements of her history and put it together with incidents that happened to others to illustrate the complexities of life in a poignant and entertaining fashion. In essence, her story becomes a parable to all women of a healthy way to approach life and that it is possible to reach all your desires.

What is made clear is that the process is not always easy and that obstacles constantly crop up whether they involve you or those you are close to at work or in your family. Her story is very realistic as it constantly shows the everyday problems we all face, and then how to overcome them. It doesn't take superhuman qualities to do so. Instead, Swarna shows that common sense, wisdom, and a mindful approach to things is what will help us to overcome life's issues.

I am excited to see the next steps she takes in her life as she moves forward to help others in this new way. As a gifted doctor, Dr. Swarna has helped many through her medical expertise. I am confident that she will use her talents through this book and others, as well as personal interaction, to help many women achieve a wonderful balance in life.

Nicole Dauphinee Thessen,
News Anchor, Reporter, #1 Bestselling Author

Contents

ADVANCE PRAISE FOR *THE INTEGRATION: A TRIUMPHANT JOURNEY OF TRIALS AND ERRORS* — *i*

ACKNOWLEDGMENTS — xi

DEDICATION — xiii

FOREWORD — xv

INTRODUCTION — xix

CHAPTER 1 — 1

We come from different places; yet we are all so much the same.

CHAPTER 2 — 9

We learn from our parents how to be parents to our children… and then sometimes we have to be taking care of those parents.

CHAPTER 3 — 17

Life is a series of journeys, and I certainly enjoyed all mine.

CHAPTER 4 — 27

Change is one of the constants in life.

CHAPTER 5 — 37

Preparing for birth helps you prepare for life.

CHAPTER 6 — 45

You can tack through the winds of change brought about by a new child.

CHAPTER 7 — 49

Molding a family is worth all the effort you put into it.

CHAPTER 8   57

Having more than one child has its unique challenges.

CHAPTER 9   69

It is good to be open to whatever life brings you.

CHAPTER 10   79

The journey is always ongoing as we look for new ways to help others.

EPILOGUE   87

INTRODUCTION

It is funny how ideas take shape. My original thought with this book was to prepare a memoir of my life as a doctor who came to America at a young age to study and to realize her dream. Then I realized that I also had a great deal of practical experience as a wife and a mother to offer help to other women who struggle to be good in those roles as they also aspire to do well in their chosen profession. Finally, I began to have serious thoughts about adding to or changing my career after so many years of being a doctor. I realized that as I wrote, I wanted to take a more active interest in sharing the lessons. I started to put my experiences down on paper as I composed this book.

This book is not a memoir, though I do relate a great deal about my life. It is not a self-help book, though I want others to see that there are ways to improve how we maneuver through life. It is not a "how to" book for an immigrant coming to America, though I offer many insights on how to relish being part of a new country without giving up your identity.

At its heart, this book is a guide regarding certain concepts to make the journey through life a little easier in order to realize your dreams, desires, and goals. That is what makes life's journey so unique; it is different for everyone. When driving from Point A to Point B, there are a limited number of practical routes. Life doesn't work that way. A myriad of routes can take us to our destination. The destination itself may go through changes. What I want this book to do is begin to equip you for wherever you want to go and whatever you might encounter.

I borrow liberally from my own life experience and that of colleagues and friends to illustrate the different facets of life. While my experiences are varied, the insight I found through others sharing their life story with me are also valuable.

I hope I wrote them all down in an entertaining and informative way for the reader. I did change some names and circumstances to protect privacy, but the lessons are intact. I once heard that when you write something, you want to make your audience laugh, you want to make them cry, and you want to make them think. I hope I achieved those goals.

To say that life is busy is an understatement. Even if a person is single with no relationship or children in his or her life, time seems to fly by as you struggle to do everything you think you should. Throw into that family and managing your career, and life can seem very overwhelming. While there is no Holy Grail of a solution to navigating life, I believe I show you some practical experience that will give you tools to do just that. That is what this book strives to do.

One caveat is that things do not simply "happen." For any positive results you might realize from this book, it is necessary to mindfully apply its simple concepts and solutions. You might know how to diet, but if you do not apply the principles of healthy eating and exercise, nothing is going to happen. That is true of all I talk about. While I believe you will enjoy what you read here, it isn't going to be helpful unless you use it.

That is a tall order, I know. The story I relate here is only the beginning piece of how to navigate life with an eye towards balance and happiness. As with any journey, it all begins with a simple step. I plan on adding stories, books, and other resources to help you as I continue my own journey in helping others. I look forward to hearing your stories about how my concepts helped your life. Hearing success like that is the best "thank you" I can receive. Enjoy the book!

CHAPTER 1

We come from different places; yet we are all so much the same.

America is a land of immigrants. The only exception is the Native Americans that were here to see large ships with sails land on their shores and disgorge white men and women who would entirely turn the land they lived on upside down. As time went on, the descendants of the early settlers looked upon America as their land. They looked at the periodic waves of new immigrants coming to America with distrust. First, it was people from places like Italy, Ireland, Germany, and other European countries who made the United States their new home. Once they became established, and the resulting generations honestly felt that they were Americans, people from India, China, and other countries from Asia arrived.

With periodic changes in immigration policies and people coming from new places, there were two constants with each new wave of migration from other countries to America. One was that the newcomers had to settle in their adopted country balancing their desire to become part of their new home while wanting to keep a link to the culture they left. The second was that Americans who had been born here or lived here for a while had to make room and try to understand who the new immigrants were and what they wanted. For both immigrants and Americans, this was not always easy.

My name is Sheenu, and I am a physician living and working in Staten Island, N.Y. for a long time now. I was born in India, and the United States has been my home for decades. I have experienced the thrill of the new and the reluctance of letting go of the old. America offered many challenges for me as well as a wealth of opportunities. In truth, I still find challenges and opportunities every day. One of those challenges has always been feeling the pull of the culture and lessons I learned as a girl in India and reconciling them with my new country. America is very much my home, but you can never forget where you come from. I figured I would turn that change in my life into an opportunity and share my story with other transplanted women and men who migrated to the United States and made it their home.

I have enjoyed being part of as well as being an initiator of the integration between people resettling here from other countries with those who have been here for generations. To this day, I appreciate those that took me under their wing when I first arrived in America and for the years afterward. No handbook covers every person and their situation. However, I believe my story is something that many immigrants can relate to, and I love to help people make their lives better. I want others to learn that my philosophy of "Awareness, Assess, Adapt, Adopt, and Act" are the keys to finding contentment in their new country. As a result, you experience meaningful "aha moments" that enrich your life. I will expound on them as I continue my story.

While I believe our journey through life is endless and filled with lessons and adventures along the way, I do want to tell you where I am now on my continuing voyage. I will be sharing my story as I proceed through the chapters. However, I do think it is essential to give you a snapshot of where I am in my life now. It is difficult for an individual to figure out where they are going without seeing where they have been. I have indeed come to understand the significance of that, and I hope my continuous quest for insight will be an incentive for you to do the same.

I am happily married to my husband, Raman. He is also a physician, and one of the things we have in common is that we genuinely enjoy helping other people. Of course, in our career, that means not only helping our patients resolve physical issues but supporting them to become aware of their emotional and mental state as well. Also, we have many opportunities to channel that love of other people by volunteering to help in some cause or putting our efforts into worthwhile projects, such as this book you are reading!

We created a home full of love and warmth for our three children. Avi and Arya are working on their careers and into the dating scene as they are exploring relationships. Aru is preparing for college admission and about to embark on leaving the nest and starting out on the road to adulthood. Of course, as a mother, my kids are always a concern, and that doesn't change no matter how old everyone becomes. I believe we do our best to prepare our children to be ready to face the world when they are out of the house. If we do that job as parents, then we are doing okay!

I like the house we live in. It isn't too big nor is it too small, but it is definitely our home. I don't believe Raman and I are all that different from other couples. We enjoy being able to take vacations, going to the theatre, or dining out with friends. We like to play bridge and golf or heading out to Manhattan for the day. It is always great to get together with our friends when everyone's schedule allows. We like to socialize and be with others whether it is to go to a wine tasting or just dinner at someone's house. Walking along the oceanfront is always popular and a source of relaxation. It is also a treat to meet new people. You never know when you might make a new friend or have others introduce you to a new interest that you come to like.

For many people, we exemplify the "American dream." The concept of that has evolved over the years, but it tends to mean having a good career, family, and the means to enjoy it and do some of the things you want to do in life. I certainly have no complaints along those lines, and you can succeed by applying yourself and not being afraid to work hard. Was everything easy to get to this point in life? No, but I do not know anyone whose journey through life wasn't littered with potholes, rocks, and hills. That is what makes the traveling so interesting!

I arrived in the United States in the late seventies. After all this time, I feel that I belong here. It is my home, and I proudly support her. However, I have many thoughts and memories of the traditions of my country — India. Here is the crux that I do want to talk about in this book. I believe that when you make another country your home, it is not a black and white decision to throw out your past heritage and wholly adopt what is new. It is more like a careful process of combining the two so that at your core you are at peace with who you are. You do not want to be a stranger in a strange land, but you do want to remember your homeland.

The United States is a big melting pot almost since the first settlers came here in the 1600s. In the late 1800s and early twentieth century, many European immigrants came to this country. What was very common is that the new arrivals tended to settle in regions where their fellow countrymen or descendants of the original immigrants lived. Many times, this meant going to specific cities or areas of the country. However, you can look at how parts of New York City developed to get a picture of the situation. You had neighborhoods that became predominantly Italian, German, Irish, Russia, etc. You had areas settled through religious affiliation like Catholic, Protestant, or Jewish. New York City was a microcosm of this type of settling occurring all over the country.

Many of these people didn't give up their heritage. They merged it with American culture and adopted new traditions. In fact, American culture became a happy mix of traditions from other countries. The Irish started eating pasta and pizza. The Germans shopped in Polish food stores. Perhaps no one time of the year shows the melding of cultures as much as Christmas. For Americans that celebrate Christmas, they do so through traditions taken from many different countries. From the Christmas tree to sending out greeting cards, an American Christmas is an amalgamation of what other nations brought to the United States.

Today, we have people arriving in the country from all over Asia, Africa, and different Hispanic countries. People still tend to gravitate to an area where they have family and friends from their own country as immigrants did in the past. Communities spring up that have a massive ethnic flair for a particular region or country of the world. Like the first wave of immigrants, today's newcomers spend a great deal of time trying to figure out how to marry the new country with their customs. Just as the European immigrants discovered decades ago, it isn't always easy.

When I arrived here, I ran into a lot of what I just related. You do feel like the proverbial fish out of water, but you can soon begin to feel yourself adapting and feeling like you belong. To this day, there were aspects of the United States I thought were terrific and I love today. Coming from India, I find the sense of independence particularly attractive. My children can go and become anything they want. The opportunity is certainly here in this country to apply yourself in any career direction you desire. The educational prospects are boundless, and you can speak your mind on any subject.

I also love how America is that big melting pot. As I mentioned, this country has seen various waves of new people calling the United States their home. This diversity and being able to learn different cultures makes America an exciting place. There aren't too many countries where if you wanted to find out how people lived in an area like Vietnam, all you have to do is invite your neighbors from across the street over for dinner. They can bring a dish of Vietnamese food, and you can talk the night away about where you each came from before settling in America.

As with most things in life, nothing is perfect. I still have to adjust periodically to the free flow of emotions and communications between people. I am not sure if it is my heritage, upbringing, or personality, but listening to others at times borders on TMI (too much information). Conversely, I also run into some people who insist on too much formality. This could be with a personal contact or just trying to get something done in my kids' school, for example. While America is a melting pot, not everything has the same melting temperature. Our country certainly has its contradictions!

On the other hand, I am perfectly happy here. I feel like my family and I have successfully integrated into American society while keeping our heritage and traditions as part of our lives. After all, my children were born here, but they are still very cognizant and respectful of their culture. The kids have had grandparents, uncles, aunts, and cousins visit them here in the United States. They have also traveled to India over the years.

I believe my children epitomize what it means to be a first-generation American. They are very proud of their Indian heritage and proud to be an American. They have acquired a very global view of people and just how diverse we are as a country and as a world. What I am thrilled about with them is that they are very comfortable in their own skin and with whom they are.

I feel the same way. America has been my home for a long time, and I have embraced her values. I love the ideology of being an American. The United States has been my home and allowed me to nurture my family, career, and other aspirations. It is so "American" to take the time to reflect on my life and then take those lessons and help others. The values and opportunities of the USA make bringing this book to others possible.

I am also grateful for growing up in India and how that helped prepare me for my life in another country. India is a diverse country with different cultures and religious beliefs. I also had a somewhat liberal upbringing, and it equipped me to have a great mindset in America. I grew up around people speaking different languages. No matter their background, I learned to adapt to who they were and their country of origin. The bottom line is that I could embrace them as my friends.

Having these friends from different cultures helped to expose me to people from different ethnicities. Getting to know them enabled me to nurture my thirst for knowledge that always seemed to be part of me. I wanted to know more about my friends as I grew up and what their customs and heritage entailed. I know it helped me to love my friends and certainly aided me as I adapted to life in the United States with the various people I met in school and my professional capacity.

Besides what I learned from growing up in India, I met many people in this country that helped me in adjusting to a new country. Throughout my schooling here, and even into my residency, I met many people from other countries. We were all in the same boat by being in a new country, and there were a camaraderie and support that were unique. Ultimately, we were all human beings celebrating each other's cultures as we worked towards establishing ourselves in our adopted country.

This is how I found myself after many years in the United States. I had my family, and I had my career. I was very content with life, although I was thinking about different ways of how I wanted to help others beyond my medical practice. All seemed right with the world. Then, one evening when I was sitting down with my family to dinner, the phone rang.

CHAPTER 2

We learn from our parents how to be parents to our children...
and then sometimes we have to be taking care of those parents.

Telephones have this ability to change your life the moment you answer a call. It could be great news like being offered a new job. The flip side of the coin is that it can be something terrible. That was the type of phone call I received that night at dinner. My mother was in ICU in a hospital in India.

After hanging up the phone, my husband could tell something was wrong. I was gripping the edge of a table, and he could see the anguish that washed over my face. I shared with him what I just heard and together we started making plans. I was going to go to India on the first available flight. This meant making arrangements for my patients since I wasn't sure how long I would be gone. There were several things to take care of while I was away. All in all, it was a whirlwind of a time, and I couldn't have done it myself. I have always been grateful for the partnership I had with Raman, and it made what we had to do in a short amount of time go as smoothly as possible.

I am still not sure how, but I was soon on a flight to India. With the prospect of a 16-hour trip ahead of me, I forced myself to sit back and tried to relax. It was not easy. As a physician, I could usually keep my mind clear and focus on the problem at hand. While I believe I form great connections with my patients, having something happen to a family member can make any orderly mind sputter and go in varied directions. This is especially true when it is an immediate family member like a parent, sibling, or child. Having watched all those situations happen to others and feeling their pain, it still does not prepare you for when it happens to you.

Many thoughts went through my mind during that long plane ride. One of the first thoughts I had was this was something everybody fears when they leave their family and travel to live in another country. What if a family member gets very sick or worse while you are so far away? Equally fearful is when you think about yourself becoming ill so far away from family. I am not saying this is one of those paralyzing thoughts at the forefront of your mind every day, but it is always there lurking somewhere in the background. Part of it is that you know nobody is going to stay healthy and live forever. It has not happened yet! We hope those occasions might be 30, 40, and 50 years in the future, but you never know. As a doctor, I face that regularly when treating my patients.

Having that understanding still didn't prepare me for the shock of hearing my mother was in the Intensive Care Unit. As a doctor, I was trying to prepare myself for what I found, what questions to ask, find out what medications she was on, and were they going to recommend any procedures. As a daughter, I just wanted my mom to be okay.

I have learned through observation that there is no one way to be a parent. At this point in my life, I have experienced my parents and those of my friends. As a mother, I am a parent, and you know that you do not do parenting the same way that a friend or colleague would. Of course, you come into contact with your children's friends and their parents. Sometimes, it is with the jarring, "Sally's parents would let her to this!" — whatever the "this" at the time was. We all learn to parent like we do most things in life — by trial and error. Are Raman and I perfect parents? We probably like our children to think so, but the truth is we all make mistakes. When you learn from your mistakes and take positive ideas you see other parents doing and apply them, then you are far ahead on the parenting curve.

I found myself thinking about this as my mind wandered back to growing up in India. My younger sister and I were fortunate to grow up in a family where our parents were liberal minded and forward thinking. In hindsight, I realize my mom and dad wanted us to take responsibility for our lives. They concentrated on my sister and I being able to grow and thrive as adults. They taught us that girls could grow up to be anything they want. My parents did not present any gender boundaries to us. While they prepared us for the adult world, it wasn't like they were eager to have us leave home. They loved my sister and me very much, but I believe they were conscious of preparing us to be on our own. As parents, that is our most significant role. We want our kids to be ready to leave the nest. As a parent, the paradox of the parenting role is that if we do our job very well, the kids will fly the nest.

This becomes a blind spot for some mothers and fathers as they cannot bear the thought of their children going away. It can make for some bad parental decisions. However, if you do the job correctly, the kids will create their independent lives, but their connection to you will continue to be strong. The geographic proximity is all that changes.

I certainly felt that way about my parents too. They prepared me so well that I was able to go thousands of miles away to another country to train for my career and to eventually start a family. Many kids at that age are agonizing about going a couple of hundred miles away to college.

We were far from each other, but that didn't mean I didn't have their support in my new country. There were phone calls and letters. Today, it is even more comfortable with real-time texting, emails, Skype, social media, and every new way of communicating that seems to be invented on a monthly basis. It can almost sound like you are living the next town over from your family instead of a couple of continents away.

I know every immigrant does not have a family support system back in their native country. Some people are refugees, and some leave because of a break in the family. However, those that have strong family ties do not have to abandon those relationships because they moved away. Some people eventually bring their family over to America with them. This can present a complex learning experience of new land with all family members involved, but at least everyone is together.

I think my experience has taught me how to handle the long-distance family relationships. We could travel to India on trips, and our children often came with us when they became part of the picture. Both of our parents and various other relatives came to visit us in the United States. When you have the means to do this, it has beneficial results for everybody. Our parents could see and experience where we lived and what we did instead of only having to hear about it from me and trying to imagine it. I could keep in touch with people and places I knew when I visited over there. Just as importantly, my children got to know their grandparents and experienced some of their heritage right in India. I believe everyone appreciated about each other's lives a little more on these visits.

Even if you cannot visit regularly, it is essential to stay in touch as frequently as possible. The key to any relationship whether it is with your significant other, your children, your parents, work colleagues, etc. is communication. Generally, the cause of any falling out between people, or just drifting apart, is lack of communication. As I mentioned, it is easier now than ever before. It only takes a little effort on everyone's part to reach out and keep in touch.

Many of these thoughts went through my mind as I flew towards India. My mother helped give me a solid foundation from which I grew. She insisted that education was important and that was a big thrust in my life. From her, I also learned what it meant to care for others and how vital it was to connect with other people. I don't believe she ever set out to teach me how to become a doctor, but her lessons in my childhood certainly shaped me.

I realized the irony during the flight that my parents' example of caring about others had me trying to get halfway around the world as quickly as I could. Now I was trying to grapple with the facts that might be in front of me when I arrived in India. I knew that being in the ICU of a hospital is taxing on family members. However, I didn't have all the facts in front of me yet. I wasn't sure of her condition or what she would need when she came out of the hospital. My thoughts went to my father and how he was handling all of this. With all the medical advice and knowledge that I dispensed to my patients and their families, I was out of my comfort zone here. I had to start thinking about how I was going to handle this situation.

You know, it doesn't matter if you are living in another country and a parent gets sick because you still have your career and family responsibilities. And yes, being seven thousand miles away adds complications, but the other factors still come into play if your parents live in the next town from you.

Thoughts were racing in and out of my mind. There is a reason why it is good to learn meditation or some other practice to calm down the brain. If you do not have some discipline over your thoughts, times of stress can send it in so many different directions at once that it is hard to focus on the problem at hand. I was having a little of this going on as I was sitting in my seat.

I tried to turn my thoughts away from what I didn't know and instead focus on what I did. First, I reminisced a great deal about growing up in India. I thought about all the good times I had with my mother. It seemed like every story I thought about, I could see a connection to some facet of my adult life. I felt her influence on me whether I was brand new to the United States or trying to make my way through college.

As I thought about my mom, my dad came into those different memories as well. I reflected on how our experiences condition us for future. I watched my mother and father over the years go through all the ups and downs of married life. The bottom line is that they loved each other and their goal was to be there for their children.

Thinking about them had me hoping that Raman and I were good role models for our kids in what a relationship should be. My two older ones are exploring that stage in life right now. I realized that preparing them to be adults, as my parents did for me, meant more than having an appreciation for education, hard work, and having a sense of integrity in all that they do. It also meant being an example of how to care about others and how to be there for the other person when you enter into a relationship with someone.

As I kept progressing from one thought to another, I now found myself thinking about Raman. With Raman, I found a fantastic life mate and partner. We have been married for a while now, and our affection for each other has only grown. I didn't have to think much further back than before I got on this plane for how he is always there for me. I knew whatever details I missed during the craziness to get ready for this trip would be covered by him while I was gone.

When we got married, the key was that we addressed our family responsibilities together. This meant we discussed matters that concerned budgets, kids, home repairs, buying a new car — pretty much everything. We are not two people anymore when we marry; we are one unit.

I also had the confidence that he was only a phone call or text away when I got on the ground. As you can imagine, two doctors in the same house can add its own brand of stress to a relationship in addition to the regular craziness of raising three children. I believe we have been successful in raising our family. When I think about the nervous teenage girl who arrived in America and where she is now with career and family, I can only marvel. Raman has been a big part of me, and we have successfully navigated all those potential reefs a marriage can encounter. I am not sure how much my parents' relationship was an influence on me, but I know it was a supportive factor.

I wished Raman could make this journey with me. Still, it was a relief knowing he was taking care of things back home. It has been great having such a good connection in our relationship from the beginning. It seemed to be that way from when we met and all through our marriage. We make a good team. By definition, a team is a group of people who work well together to achieve a common goal. When I think about that, I know we make a good team. That goes from forming objectives to figuring out how to accomplish them and then implementing the plan. I doubt that we met many of our objectives by traveling a straight line. There were always bumps and curves and sudden turns we didn't expect. However, we did most of the things we set out to do. We are two people who work well together.

My thought went from that to another time in my life when I had to rush to a hospital for a family member. A shiver caressed my spine as I thought back to that occasion.

CHAPTER 3

Life is a series of journeys, and I certainly enjoyed all mine.

One of the wonders of being in med school is how you learn the science and skills to help make a person feel better or to save their life. The challenge is realizing that you cannot save everyone. Sometimes you are thrust into the position of hitting dead ends when you are trying to diagnose a patient. I learned about this early on in my career while I was still in school.

My mother, sister, and I were at the movies. I was in med school, and it was a rare night out. My little sister was only in second or third grade and, as I think back to that time, we were all so young. We were watching a Bollywood movie with a great deal of singing and dancing. I remember distinctly that we were listening to a song with the line, "You have to compromise in life," when someone came into the theatre looking for us.

To this day, I am not sure who tracked us down and how they found us. You have to remember, this is before the days of cell phones and instant communication. Whoever it was rushed to tell us that my father was in severe pain and at the urgent care facility near our home.

We rushed out of the theatre. My mother and I dropped my sister off at a friend's home since we didn't know what was going on and raced to my father. We found him in a great deal of discomfort. It seemed to be in his abdomen area, but the staff at the urgent care weren't sure how to treat him. They called for an ambulance.

I told my mother and the ambulance personnel in no uncertain terms that I was going with my father in the ambulance. My mother ran home to pick up a checkbook, some clothes, and other things for my dad. Again, this was several years ago, and the world was not like today where you could use a credit card to cover expenses everywhere, let alone a hospital. She gathered up anything she thought my father would need and met us at the emergency room.

The ride to the hospital is etched into my memory. The ambulance attendants did what they could to make my father comfortable. I remember the siren and the flashing lights as we made our way through the streets. All I could do was hold his hand and say things like, "It will be okay. We will find out what is wrong." This had nothing to do with my medical training to that point. It had everything to do with being a daughter and loving my father.

I believe this was my first experience where it dawned on me that doctors do not have all the answers. Unfortunately, it had to concern my father. The doctors did all manner of tests, but they weren't coming up with anything concrete that they could treat. In the meantime, my father was still in terrible pain, and my mother was very upset.

It was at that point that I decided to assert myself. I was only at the beginning of my medical studies, so I wasn't going to solve the diagnosis myself. However, I knew where I could go for help.

What I ended up doing was getting on the phone and calling one of my professors. He impressed me in class, and I had a feeling he was more experienced than the doctors working on my father were at that point in their careers. I begged him for his help. To my relief, he said he would. He listened to the doctors about my father's symptoms and instructed them to run a couple of other tests. The short version is that they finally discovered that the severe pain was due to a duodenal ulcer that had ruptured. Finally, they took him to the operating theatre for surgery.

After successful surgery, my father started feeling better. I am forever grateful for that professor stepping in and lending a hand. As doctors, that is precisely what we are supposed to do, and he was a great example of professional ethics.

I learned a few things from that experience. The first is that medical science, like all sciences, is continually changing with new discoveries, techniques, and information. As doctors, we must keep on top of it as best we can, but it can become overwhelming. That is why the second thing I learned is that we always must be aware of the resources available to us. I know there are still going to be people that are going to be more knowledgeable than me on specific subjects because of education and experience. Experienced people could be a resource for me. Likewise, I am open to being a resource for others when needed.

That experience also gave me insights about myself. I found out I certainly was capable of taking charge when I had to. Maybe the doctors at the hospital would have eventually found the problem or called one of their mentors for help. I don't know, but seeing my father suffering spurred me to action. It did make an impression on me that taking charge didn't mean I had to solve the problem. Sometimes being in charge is all about bringing the right people on board that can resolve the issue at hand.

After that experience, I recognized education wasn't all about books, lectures, labs, and exams. They were important, and I worked diligently at them, but I also realized the value of common sense and experience. I knew the experience would come, and I would mindfully learn everything I could from events and people that came across my path.

Soon after my schooling finished, it was time to embrace life and my career. At the time, the life part was easy. Raman and I were a young husband and wife, and we had fun! Being a newly married couple with both of us in the medical profession, we weren't that much different than any other young couple. First of all, we were very much into each other. We wanted to be together. We wanted to explore each other and figure out how to make this marriage thing work. It was a journey that continues to this day. Maybe that is the secret to a good marriage — you can't give up on each other, and you have to realize it is a continuous process.

Like many other newlyweds, we didn't have a great deal of money. This happens to anyone starting out in a career, even medicine. I think one problem young people have is that they see successful people in the career they pursue, and they aspire to that. There is nothing wrong with that motivation, but sometimes a young man or woman forgets that even the most successful had to start somewhere. Rarely does anyone begin near the top of a profession. Almost everyone has to start at the lower ends of the career ladder and work their way up.

That is where Raman and I were at the beginning of our marriage. We were both beginning our lives together and our careers. Raman was a couple of years ahead of me in establishing himself as a physician, but it was still new to him. We didn't let that, or the scarcity of money, slow us down.

We loved to travel, and still do! We made the decision that we would do as much traveling as possible when we were young within our money constraints. The key is to have a budget and stick to it. We were going to enjoy life, but we made the decision not to go into debt while doing it. That would be my advice to any young couple today — don't go into debt. With the ease of access to credit, it is hard not to be tempted to do something now and worry about paying for it later. Debt is challenging to overcome, and the best way to deal with it is to avoid it!

We had a grand time back then and on a budget. We had a car, and the United States was a vast, beautiful country waiting for us to explore it. The country has many natural wonders, and quite a few man-made ones. With maps in hand (no GPS back in the day) and not a significant amount of money in our pockets, we went exploring every chance we had. Sometimes it was day trips around where we lived; other times were long journeys of exploration.

I remember one trip we took through the West. We wanted to see the Grand Canyon. It is one of those natural wonders of America that you never tire of looking at when you are there. The vastness and the beauty of its landscape are overwhelming. Photos don't do it justice, and as you are looking at the different vistas and animals that are around, you can't get enough of it. It was certainly worth the trip.

When we went to find a room for the night, we came across a small motel, and they had one room left. As we stood in the little lobby debating if we could afford the thirty dollars, a couple with a child came in looking for a place for the night. They looked exhausted and spent from a long day. When the person behind the desk said we had taken the last room, Raman and I looked at each other and gave it to the couple. We smiled at them and told them to enjoy their night. We got in our car and decided to head the several hundred miles to Las Vegas.

Here was another life lesson. We were tired too and looked forward to the intimacy of a night together. However, when we saw that couple and child, we knew they needed it more than we did. I think it was so important that we gave them the room with a smile and good wishes. I believe that is how we need to go through life. Sometimes you need to do things that make you uncomfortable or require sacrifice. Do it with a smile and a good heart. You can call it fate or karma or whatever, but you do get back what you put out.

We had a lot of fun and adventures on our trips. We certainly met many different people. When we were in Vegas on that same trip, we were walking around one of the big hotels looking at all the glitz and the vastness of the place. While we were looking out over the casino, a couple came up to us. They started telling us about how they had all their money stolen, and now they were looking for help to be able to afford bus tickets back to Los Angeles. They focused on Raman and continued elaborating on all the tragedy and bad people they ran into since arriving in Las Vegas.

Their story was heartrending, but I sensed they were not telling the truth. The fit of their clothes was too good, and their story seemed … well … rehearsed. Raman looked at me in a way that I knew he thought as I did. He tried to excuse himself, but the couple only got more plaintive about their troubles. I excused myself to the ladies' room and immediately looked for security. In a Las Vegas casino, that isn't hard to find. Quickly, a couple of gentlemen came over to Raman and the couple. When the couple saw who was coming, they tried to leave, but the security men grabbed their arms and escorted them away. The woman gave me a very mean look. I smiled.

We were asked to go to the security office to file a complaint, which we did. There, the chief of security for the hotel said that a report had circulated around Las Vegas of a couple doing what they tried on us — conning others out of their money. He couldn't arrest them since nobody had filed criminal charges, but now their picture could be circulated. The couple knew no casino in the city would welcome them at all. The security chief thanked us for our help and for the presence of mind to come and get someone. He also gave us a room for a couple of nights as a thank you. We got to stay for free in a very nice hotel we wouldn't have been able to afford otherwise!

We had other adventures as we traveled around the USA. For all the places we saw, a great deal of the enjoyment of traveling is the people you meet. For a country as big as America, there is such a variety of accents, ideals, outlooks on life, etc. It certainly enriched our lives to meet people from all sections and all walks of life. I believe it certainly helped in my career as a doctor. When you care about your patients, it is easier to talk to them when you have a feeling for where they come from and what they have experienced.

Many of our travels happened around the places where we worked. We moved a few times as Raman found positions in different cities. At one point, we relocated to Memphis, Tennessee. I was done with school and looking for a place to do my residency. I was honored and ecstatic to find a place at St. Jude.

St. Jude Children's Research Hospital is one of the leading institutions for understanding, treating, and defeating childhood cancer and other life-threatening diseases. I love children. When I was in medical school and first became a doctor, I intended to work with children. I wanted to be a pediatrician and started shaping my career path in that direction. To land at a place like St. Jude was a dream come true and seemed like a huge stepping-stone. I would be able to help children and work with some of the most exceptional professionals.

It was everything I hoped it would be. It is great whenever you can work with the top talent in one of the best institutions in your field. My profession revolved around hospitals, not companies, but you get the concept. I learned so much in my time there. I did enjoy working with the children and interacting and counseling the parents. I had the opportunity to work with and observe doctors and other medical professionals at the top of their game. There are lessons I learned from back then that I use to this day.

When you are in a medical residency as a new doctor, the hospital or facility you are at rotates you through their different departments. St. Jude was no different, and at one point I was working with the young cancer patients. This became a turning point in my career.

It is almost impossible to meet anyone who has not been touched by cancer. A person has either dealt with the disease or knows a family member or close family friend who has. Cancer has reached its ugly fingers into almost every family in America in some form. After all the years I have been a doctor, we have got better at dealing with specific types of cancer, but we still have a long way to go.

I think some of the bravest patients I have met are the children battling cancer. They are so young and have no life perspective in which to understand what is going on. They have doctors and nurses sticking them with needles, trying different treatments, and working to make them more comfortable. I still marvel at the sight of a five-year-old dragging his IV bottle behind her as she is trying to play with another child. They only want to be kids and are not going to let a disease they don't understand be in their way.

As a doctor, I truly care and want to help my patients. I found when working with children that I became closer to them than I probably would with an adult. I couldn't help it. You want them to like you and relate to you so that it is easier to find out how they are feeling and to treat them.

There was one cancer patient I became very close to at St. Jude. She was a little girl named Susan, and we became buddies. Not a day went by when I was on the floor that we didn't talk and giggle together. She had a tough fight against the disease, but like so many children I met, she seemed to dig down and tolerated all the treatments we were doing to try and help her.

One night as I was about to leave for home, Susan called out to me. She looked more tired than usual and seemed down. She looked up at me and held out her hand. I took it, and she asked me, "Am I going to get better?"

I was not quite prepared for that, but I hugged her and said, "Yes, you will, sweetheart. You get some sleep, and I will see you in the morning."

When I came in the next day and went over to her, the bed was empty. Susan had died in the night. It seemed to leave a hole in my heart.

CHAPTER 4

Change is one of the constants in life.

We all have those moments described as "life-defining." They do not fit into any one category. One person might hear a piece of fantastic music and aspire to be a great musician. Someone else might enjoy learning about math and science and move forward to be an accomplished scientist. A soldier might be changed forever by the carnage he witnessed on the battlefield. For me, it was an empty bed.

It isn't easy being a doctor. I am not even talking about the schooling and the accumulated knowledge we have to learn and then keep current with during our career. As much as you must be professional and sometimes develop a sense of detachment from your patients, the truth is that I am not working on an automobile. I am working with people and want to do everything possible to cure them or make their life better with whatever ails them.

Seeing the empty bed where that sweet, little girl was before I went home the previous night made me think. Did I want to pursue a direction in medicine that would place me in the position of working with many children where I might lose more than I save? Even with all our medical breakthroughs and techniques, diseases like cancer still hold the upper hand many times. We are always getting better at battling it, but it is far from being eradicated.

It comes down to a personal choice when you are a doctor. Some individuals put themselves out there fighting diseases to try and make a difference. We all handle a loss of a patient differently. Some can control their emotions and thoughts in a way so they can keep moving through the tragedies that are inevitable. These doctors are not callous by any means. I admire them for continuing as they keep trying to make a difference in those that are sick.

At this time in my life, I was only in my early twenties, newly married, and I was seriously discussing with Raman about starting a family. Two young doctors having kids might not have been the most logical discussion we could have then, but when you are young and in love, logic tends to go out the window. I believe I have the same strong maternal urges as any young woman, and I cannot deny that probably factored into my feeling of devastation when I discovered Susan died.

Even though I couldn't put a name on it at the time, this was probably the first time I went through the mental and emotional process of the 5 A's: Awareness, Assess, Adapt, Adopt, and Act. When you do all these steps, your response is usually another "A" — Aha! It is something I refined over the years and love to share with others, but trying to ascertain what direction I wanted to take my career was the beta test for developing such a philosophy. It isn't a difficult thing to do, but it does take mindfulness to apply to situations in your life when you first use it. After a while, though, it becomes part of you, and you find yourself going through the steps of the 5 A's as naturally as breathing.

First of all, it is a mental and emotional process. Many people try to look at a situation as coldly and logically as possible. This might be okay if you are in a lab trying to figure out a new chemical compound that will hold steel together or constructing a dismantled jet, but for decisions that affect your life, you have to bring your heart and mind together. They do not act independently of each other. Of course, you have to learn how to keep a balance of the two as you think through a situation. Too much emotion can cloud your logical thinking. Conversely, not listening to your emotions might also fog your vision. Many people have great instincts when they tap into their feelings. As a friend of mine once told me, "If I always listened to my gut, I would have made the right decision 95 percent of the time in my life. Unfortunately, I only have a 50 percent success rate because there were times when I overthought something."

Awareness of this situation is that I didn't see myself spending my life working with children only to have to go through sometimes losing them. Susan hit me like a punch in my gut and created an emptiness inside. I couldn't shake it off. Here I was in one of the leading children's hospitals in the country and working with some of the best medical people in the field. I loved that opportunity, and I certainly enjoyed working with the kids and their families. Everybody was there to help a child become well.

While I am sure I would celebrate every boy and girl who turned the corner to a healthy life, I did not know if I could take the setbacks. Since I now have the gift of hindsight and experience, I might have been able to learn to cope. Since I was not quite 25 years old yet at the time, I didn't feel like finding out if I could devote my life to working with children in the pediatric field.

While studying, medical students encounter different specialties of medicine. During that time, many students decide on a specialty of medicine because the field interests them. Some because they found their calling in a particular area that they liked, and others because a student decided on what he or she did not want to do.

With awareness comes freedom in knowing that you have to decide something. Many of us get that feeling of being "stuck" in a situation — a relationship, a career, rooting for a continually losing baseball team, whatever. A big part of awareness is determining if you are truly stuck with something or if you have options. I think most of the time there are options. We only have to make ourselves honestly aware of the circumstances and where we can go to change things.

I became aware that I needed to rethink what specialty I wanted to pursue in medicine. That was a seminal moment for me and led to assessing the different parameters of what kind of doctor I wanted to be.

Assess means figuring out all aspects of a potential decision. It is not as easy as making up a pro and con list of what a particular choice would mean to you. You have to first assess yourself. Then when you look at a possible course of action, a pro and con list will have a great deal of logic and validity behind it.

Taking a hard, honest look at ourselves is one of the most difficult things we can do. We all have different issues we concentrate on when looking at ourselves. One person might look in the mirror and believe she is pretty but puts herself through a wringer trying to figure out if she is a good mother. That person's sister might think the complete opposite of herself when she goes through the same mental exercise. In reality, they are both beautiful and good moms, however, their perceptions of themselves are so different. That is why when you are assessing yourself; you honestly need to do it without any judging.

When you can do an accurate assessment of yourself, the situation, and the options, then you have to mentally adapt to the course of action you decide to take. Depending on the situation, your decision might be radically different than anything you thought about before, but you cannot be wishy-washy about it. At the least, you need to approach it with a 100 percent commitment to give yourself the best chance of succeeding. The solution you choose might not work, of course, but you gave it your best shot. If that happens, then you repeat the process, but now you have a new piece of vital information. Your original solution didn't work, and you can discard that option.

There's a familiar story that circulates about "success and failure." The story goes that Thomas Edison failed more than 1,000 times when trying to create the light bulb. (The story also can say that the attempts number 5,000 or 10,000 times depending on the version.) When asked about it, Edison allegedly said, "I have not failed 1,000 times. I have successfully discovered 1,000 ways NOT to make a light bulb."

We go through that process of finding what works for us in all facets of our life. Sometimes, it is an easy process; other times, it can be quite difficult.

Once you have adopted a certain mindset, then it is time to put in motion everything you can do to make it happen. It might mean research, talking with people you trust, and setting up a timetable to make it happen. Again, the mechanics of adopting your decision is going to vary depending on a person's tendencies. Some will do the minimum planning and scheduling to make it happen; others will go into excruciating detail. Either extreme has their dangers of preventing success. Too little information and planning can plunge someone into a situation where they make mistakes because they did not have enough details of what the solution to their problem entailed. For others, there is a "paralysis by analysis" since they believe they can never have enough information. What ends up happening is that they never move forward with their solution because they want to make sure everything is "just right."

There is a middle ground where you have the proper amount of knowledge and a decent time frame to implement your decision. This part of the process gets easier the more you do it. The bottom line is that it is time to act. You take on your solution and invest yourself totally in it. You give it your best effort. If an obstacle arises, you deal with it. If at all possible, you figure out how to go through it, around it, or over it. Nothing happens overnight, and some things we do might take longer than others in deciding if we are on the right track or not.

As I have discovered, when I go through the 5 A's, I am usually rewarded with an aha moment. This is when I feel the combination of joy, freedom, and exhilaration coming together in my emotions to know I arrived at a good solution or decision. When you feel the aha moment, you see the process did one of three things for you. One is that you made an excellent choice and the path you put yourself on is precisely the one for you. The second is that things are okay, and you will give it some more time, but you might start to explore some other options. The last is that you made a terrible choice and you have to decide on a different solution right away, thus, going through the entire 5 A's process again.

I went through this in deciding my future as a physician. I believe it works for most decisions we make in life. I have used it time and again in many different situations. It helps me make intelligent decisions utilizing my mind and emotional intelligence. Even when the choice I made did not work out completely, I choose to look at it the same way as Edison did with the light bulb — that wasn't quite the answer so I will look for another way. Setbacks in what we want to do in life aren't failures; they are only speedbumps!

When I came to terms with the idea that pediatrics was not for me, I had to decide what I wanted to do. It took some time, but the idea of working in the field of rehabilitation medicine intrigued me. I thought my aptitude for caring for my patients would be beneficial in helping them work their way through the tough experience that the road to recovery usually is. Rehab is a field that requires a physiatrist to collaborate with other physicians, which may include primary care physicians, orthopedic surgeons, neurologists, and possibly many others. It also means teaming up with other medical professionals such as occupational therapists, physical therapists, social workers, nurses, speech therapists, etc. The entire team focuses on the patient as a whole person, not just the pain or the problem area, to better help the patient and family deal with the problem physically and emotionally. The joint effort is intended to encourage and motivate the patient to optimize his or her care and ensure the best recovery possible. The more I thought about doing that work, the more I felt a sense of inner peace and calmness rise up inside of me. Emotionally and logically, it seemed like the correct course of action.

I found a location to do a residency in rehabilitation. The issue was that it wasn't in Tennessee near St. Jude. It was hundreds of miles away in Staten Island! Raman had only been at his job for ten months, and now I had to talk to him about uprooting everything again and moving for me to enroll in my opportunity.

These are the times that test any marriage or any relationship for that matter. I used to think that it was harder to do this type of discussion when the love is new, and the relationship did not have time to form a firm foundation. With the wisdom of being older, it doesn't matter. Making a tough decision isn't easier with time. Together you weigh out what balances for both of you as a couple and as individuals. The potential for a tragic conflict is there as one person's ego or selfishness could raise its head and torpedo any mutual solution that will work for both of you.

I have to say that Raman and I worked through rather easily about where I needed to go with my career. Where I thought he might have difficulty with wanting to leave because he had only been working with his new physician group for less than a year, he looked at it as not having been there long enough to set down any roots or attachments. He figured he could start over again and it would be easier because he just did it in Memphis. Raman also realized that after my epiphany at St. Jude, we would have a better chance of establishing ourselves some place different such as Staten Island.

With his support, we were on our way to New York. For the uninitiated, Staten Island is one of the five boroughs of New York City. Unlike the other four — Manhattan, Queens, Brooklyn, and the Bronx — Staten Island is totally different. It doesn't have the tall buildings or the congestion you think of when you think of New York City. It is laid out more like any city's suburbs. It has many single-family homes and apartment buildings. The homes are close together, and you do not have houses with a lot of land around them. Many families have lived there for several generations, and their heritage is that of the immigrants coming to America in the waves of people that arrived in the late 19th century into the 20th.

This was the place Raman and I determined to make our new home. We had different obstacles to overcome. Professionally, we had to prove ourselves in our new workplaces. It was not like we had years of experience as physicians. However, I do not think our trepidation about entering new hospitals and offices was any different from anyone else starting a new job. We got to know our colleagues, became familiar with new procedures, and learned about the people in the area. It was all part of the learning process.

Professionally, I found my calling in the rehabilitation area. From my first day working in this field on Staten Island, I felt as if I took to it like a duck to water. I enjoyed working with my patients, I was able to help many of them, and I found myself continually keeping up with what was current in the field. When you discover your niche in life, you rarely feel that going to work is a chore. You look forward to your next day at the office.

Living on Staten Island was a different type of adjustment. For an area of immigrants, they were not quite used to people from India at that time. I wouldn't say Raman and I were a novelty, but there weren't many Indian families in the area yet. We found that we had to use all our experience at assimilating into a new area from our past experiences of moving. New Yorkers are a unique breed, but we made friends and eventually felt like we belonged. It doesn't happen overnight, but when you mentally prepare yourself for the long haul and make an effort to meet new people, it all comes together eventually.

We were doing well in adapting to the area we moved to, the people, and our jobs. Everything was new to me, and I was enjoying getting to know the staff, learning more about my new calling, and exploring New York City with my husband. Whenever we had time to discover more of the city, we took it. Even for two busy medical professionals, we made sure that we made time for each other, and New York always had something for us to do.

All of this was going very well. At one point, I noticed some things changing with my body. As a physician, I certainly had my suspicions, but a good doctor knows to see a doctor if needed, so I made an appointment with mine.

As I was sitting in the examining room after the doctors and nurses finished all their procedures, the doctor came back in after a few minutes. The smile told me all I needed to know as the doctor said, "You are right. You're pregnant!"

CHAPTER 5

Preparing for birth helps you prepare for life.

The words brought joy to my heart. Raman and I were going to have a baby! We were a couple who wanted to have a family. My family was vital to me growing up. Indeed, it still is today. My connections with family kept me going through many difficult times in my life — both in India and when I moved to the United States. Family experiences shape us into who we are. For some, that can add to difficulties as the years pass; for many, it is a good foundation from which a person can grow. I definitely fit into the latter category, and I loved that we were bringing a child into the world.

A child illustrates the love and commitment of a couple. Raman was as happy as I was. The excitement of all these new beginnings became almost overwhelming. We were beginning new careers, and we were starting our family. I am sure you can understand the excitement and elation we were feeling.

There was also fear of becoming a mother and becoming responsible for a tiny angel. Most of the time when we face a challenge in life, whether good or bad, the fear dragon raises its head. When we are growing up, we see mothers and their children all the time. I am not sure if I ever thought it was easy, but it always looked so natural. I am sure I had the same thought any new mother has even before their son or daughter is born: "Just how do I do this?"

You discover that the parenting thing might not be as natural as you thought. I was a doctor and knew all about the physical development of a child in the womb as well as the mechanics of giving birth. I quickly discovered that didn't necessarily mean I had magical in-depth knowledge of caring for a baby. Maternal instinct does not equal complete information of what to do when the baby gets here.

The reality of the situation began to hit me as the pregnancy progressed. I was working hard to become a skilled physician in my newly chosen field of rehabilitation. The life of a resident isn't comfortable. It entails long hours and never-ending days of treating and working with patients. It provides invaluable knowledge and experience but it kind of turns into an endurance test and a marathon. Pregnancy turns into a nine-month marathon of its own and doing that and a residency is not easy.

It also began to dawn on me that I was going to be a working mother soon after my child was born. I had no plans to stop being a doctor after all the hard work I did to get to this point. Already my life with Raman had endured a great deal as we completed school and moved around completing our residencies. It seemed to us that Staten Island and the greater New York area would be our home for a time, so we embraced it with gumption. Though I had my worries and concern about the future as a working mother, we continued to have fun when we could and explored our new area. New York offers many diverse opportunities for explorations and new experiences. We are still finding new things to do today.

One thing that soon struck me is how alone we were. If I were having a baby in India, I would have had family all around from both my side and Raman's. I have talked to expectant mothers from all over in the intervening years, and that sense of being alone is prevalent if the woman is separated from family. They could be in another state or another country, but that sense of wanting family around for such a joyous and emotional occasion is universal.

I believe it is even more difficult for an immigrant coming from a culture where the family comes together to help and support a new mom and the baby for a year. Besides the natural desire of wanting family with me, I also found myself reminiscing about traditions I went through as a child in my homeland. I had never really thought about it before but with my child on the way, I began to think what he or she was going to miss by not being raised in India. I found myself getting caught up in this a bit when it struck me that it didn't have to be that way. My child was going to be born an American. Raman and I knew that the United States was our home. However, that didn't mean that my child couldn't learn and live the traditions of his or her heritage.

In the various places I lived and traveled to in the United States, it struck me how many early immigrants maintained their attachment to their heritage. It seemed that when there was any surge in immigrants from a particular country, those people started clubs and events to perpetuate their traditions. You could be Irish, Italian, or Norwegian, and you would find a place to go that remind people of their homeland. For succeeding generations, it became a way for them to learn and cherish their heritage. Today, we see more of this occurring with the recent arrivals from India, Thailand, and other Asian countries as well as Latino nations.

Like immigrants before me, I could see doing the same type of educating and having fun with my children as they learned about their Indian background. While it was only a thought at the time, I was sure there would be trips to India as well as relatives coming over here. I started to breathe easier as I could see a future where any children I had would be proud and well-versed in their roots. All of the United States is full of people who are delighted to be an American, but who are also proud to point out they are German or Brazilian or whatever country they or their parents or grandparents came from. In fact, I have seen many people whose family has been here for generations and still pridefully point to their country of origin.

While I could see the future working out well for the growth of my child, I quickly came back to my present dilemma. For most Indian immigrants, the expectant mom's mother comes to help with the preparation before the baby is born and stays for a while afterward. A beneficial part of this practice is the mom-to-be can ask her mother questions that have to do with childbirth and babies. In that way, practical information is passed down from one generation to the next. When you are having a baby, especially the first time, it is reassuring to have that knowledgeable mother on your side. It is someone you love and intimately know that helps you when becoming a new mother.

In our case, the families back home got together and decided that Ba, my mother-in-law, was the one coming over to the United States to stay with us. I have to admit that I was worried. I did not know Ba all that well. Being almost on opposite sides of the world didn't give me much of a chance to get to know her. For an act that was supposed to be helpful and reassuring for me, it added to my anxiety. How would it work with us living together? How would we interact? Would this cause more stress in an already stressful time in my life?

I learned a valuable lesson when Ba moved into our home. I discovered that any relationship could be beautiful if you stay open-minded and work at nurturing it. I wish I could say I went into the time with Ba with this mindset, but I had too much going on to think things through. However, I believe Ba did travel thousands of miles with that attitude. Whatever worries I had were soon cast aside. We got along well, and she helped prepare me for motherhood.

She was also insightful in a way that only being married for a long time can give someone. At some point, Raman and I argued. I can't even remember what it was about now, but it did happen. Ba took me aside after that and asked me, "Does it really matter who is right or wrong?" I thought about it and realized in the big picture that it didn't. This argument was not over anything major, but we got to the point where our egos didn't allow either of us to back down. When I shook my head that it didn't matter, she said, "Then don't worry about it."

It's funny how a flash of insight such as that can have a life-long impact on a person. It certainly did for me. I began to realize that sometimes arguments or fights stop being about whatever topic triggered the discussion. It can quickly deteriorate into being a battle of egos and nothing else. It helped me learn to use discernment when trying to figure out what was important when discussing something and when just to let it go.

I learned a great deal from my time with Ba. It certainly prepared me for the physical discomfort of being pregnant and when it was time to give birth. Those events have an end time and are over when the baby is born. More importantly, she gave me insight into what it meant to be a family and how to deal with different situations as they occurred. She helped both Raman and I prepare for the practical applications of being a family. We made our share of mistakes in the beginning, but she did help prevent some others.

While I became happy with Ba at home and how that was going, I had plenty of agitation with how things were doing at work. As it turned out, I didn't have to worry about that either. I had plenty of help — both during my pregnancy and when the baby arrived.

I was worried about being a working mother with all the nights I had to put in, especially as I continued my residency. I quickly learned how this was going to make me feel as I did my work while being pregnant. There is a lot to be said for what your body goes through as you have another human starting to grow inside of you. I was tired a lot. I could only imagine how this was going to affect me as I became large and closer to my due date. I also started wondering how I was going to cope when the baby was here. I realized I would be getting even less sleep then!

As my mind whirled with all these fears, a magical thing did happen to me. The staff from where I worked came together around me like a family. The beautiful thing is that my colleagues and my boss looked like a miniature version of the United Nations. We were from all over. My boss was from Ireland and the others were from the Philippines, Thailand, Cuba, and China. I probably missed a few countries in there, but I once again marveled at how people from all over can come together and not only work together but become a virtual family.

I have seen this quite frequently in my medical career. The medical profession is made up of many different nationalities. Take a walk through any hospital, and you can see this whether you are in New York City or Kansas City. People from different countries and many backgrounds work together to help people who are hurting and sick. It is nice to have a common purpose and focus on that. I believe there are other professions where the same thing happens. I often thought the people who make the most noise about immigration have no idea how people from all over can work together for the betterment of all.

I had the opportunity to live this firsthand. I had my colleagues help me when things got to be too much for me physically. They took on my night shifts, or at least parts of them. What was a dilemma turned into delight as I had more help than I thought possible. Remember, I hadn't been in my residency all that long when I became pregnant. As I look back, I think my pregnancy accelerated the process of getting to know my colleagues better. We went from cordially getting to know each other to becoming friends to turning into a family. If it took my belly getting a little bigger to become a rallying point for everyone, then so be it!

One thing I think anyone coming to the United States or going to a new country discovers is that people are people. Everyone has the same concerns, needs, and dreams. All it takes is having everyone around the staff table after an exhausting day to find out we aren't that different. Impending motherhood is undoubtedly something anybody, especially other women, can celebrate and embrace.

My supervisor was from Ireland, and she was a mother. She gave me many suggestions and a lot of advice that both reinforced things I was learning from Ba, or that complemented them. I guess then I had an insight that was profound, but silly in hindsight: a mother is a mother. It doesn't matter the race, nationality, or where you are on the economic ladder. All new mothers have the same concerns. Other mothers, whether you are related to them or not, are the best sources to calm your fears. My boss did that for me.

My pregnancy taught me a great deal about relationships. I worried about where I thought there could be a possible divergence between Ba and me. I was concerned how things would go at work. Instead, I found that there was a convergence of love and helpfulness I never anticipated. Women have many surprises during pregnancy, and some of them are quite unpleasant. I found out that life is like a great piece of music where you can have all the instruments playing together in a remarkable manner. Our job is to dance to it!

People in our lives are the instruments, and we have the privilege to watch it all come together. Sometimes the melody might be a little hard on the ears, but for the most part, it is a beautiful movement where everything flows. It took my pregnancy to discover this about others. It is a lesson I take to heart this day, and I cherish family, friends, colleagues, patients, etc. because I know that my active interaction with them will pay off in some way for all of us in the future.

To take the music analogy a little further, I do not want you to think I forgot about the most critical duet in my life. Raman was wonderful during this time. He has been great with all my pregnancies. Throughout the time leading up to the baby and beyond, we treated everything in the context of "us." It wasn't my decision or his decision about things; it was our decision. We had this mindset when we got married, and it stayed with us through the early lean times and as we became more settled in our careers. I won't speak for Raman about how he acquired his insight to be a husband, but mine as a wife came from watching my parents while growing up and then being open-minded to things Ba suggested to me. Throw in concepts I learned listening to my friends, and you can see I had some strong, positive influence in my life that helped me grow as a wife.

We were a strong team as a husband and wife. Our careers were moving along, we were making good friends, and we enjoyed and had fun in each other's company. Then we had something happen that can completely turn a married couple topsy-turvy. Our child was born.

CHAPTER 6

You can tack through the winds of change brought about by a new child.

It doesn't matter where you live or what country you came from. You can have a Ph.D. or be a high school graduate. You can be in your 20s, 30s, or 40s. You can read every book and article on childbirth and be prepared to raise that little boy or girl after they are born. You can be as prepared as humanly possible for your child coming into the world.

Then you go into the hospital to give birth, and everything you learned or think you know goes right out the window! For some, that means looking for a bigger place to live because your little studio apartment is not going to cut it with the new addition to the family. For others, you are setting up a room or area for the nursery. Then you are trying to figure out the best stroller, crib, car seat, etc. to buy. On top of that, you are thinking about clothes, diapers, pediatricians, and other concerns that you must deal with for the next 18 to 21 years!

We went through all of that and Ba was a tremendous help preparing me for being a mother. Going through the birthing process is no walk through the park, but I think I speak for many mothers and can testify that it is all worth it when you first get to hold your baby. There is a feeling of love and connection with that tiny life in your arms that will be with you the rest of your life. There is something about touching the little nose and the little fingers that nothing can replicate. The baby is your child!

Nothing turns your life upside down more than having children. For one thing, their arrival can often be at the same time when you are advancing your career! When Avi was born, I was still doing my residency in my new field related to rehabilitation. Residency for any doctor, no matter the discipline, is comparable to running a marathon while lugging a hundred-pound weight. You are trying to learn as much as you can, and you are under tremendous pressure with the hours required and the stress of working with staff and patients. It is a learning ground by fire and is pretty much a rite of passage for any doctor.

My staff rallied around me and were supportive as I worked hard at my residency requirements with my newborn. It was an exhausting and fulfilling time in my life, and I am grateful for all of those who stuck with me. Raman was a tremendous support, but he was also going through his career growing pains working in a new practice. We were excited about growing our family and careers, but that didn't mean things were not extremely stressful at times.

Having an actual baby made the pregnancy portion of residency seem like a walk in the park. I think I forgot what sleep was! I felt like I was going at a hundred miles an hour. Ba helped, but she was returning to India soon. Plus, I was a brand new mom! I read plenty of information on how to do things with a newborn, but every child is different. As I learned with the subsequent birth of my other two children, each child should come with their specific instructional manual. That's in a perfect world! In the real world, you guess and try things, keep what works, and eliminate what doesn't. Just when you think you have it down, your child changes up the rules, and you feel like you are starting over.

Don't get me wrong. In its way, raising a child is fun and indeed fulfilling. The little milestones you see in your child's life when he or she is an infant and as a toddler wipes out memories of the struggles. Life does begin to resemble a whirlwind of diapers and bottles and trying to get to work on time even though your baby spit up on you. Sleep comes in three-to-four-hour increments and you never feel rested.

Raman pitched in when he could. We worked at staying close as a couple. We would find time to laugh at the situation or figure out a way to get out on our own, even if it was to run out for an hour for a cup of tea. Love provided such a strong bond as we went through this time of our life. We loved each other, we loved our child, and we were thrilled with the idea of being a family. I believe Raman and I always looked at what we did as an adventure, whether it was when we were younger and would take road trips with barely any money, or in starting our family. I think that sense of wonder and looking to see how things were going to turn out was always part of the excitement.

I am proud to say that Avi survived being a baby, and so did we! In fact, we did so well at it, we soon brought Arya into the world, and Aru a few years after that. If you want an adventure, have enough children so that they hold a numerical advantage at home. I could write an entire book on the dynamics of having a larger family. I laugh now because sometimes a person will ask me how I did it all. While I always talk about how Raman and I accomplished it together, and we had a lot of love in the house, the truth is at the time you just did what you had to do. Yes, I worked at it closely with my husband, but when you are in the middle of the whirlwind, instinct takes over many times. Hindsight is when you can sit back, take a breath, and analyze it. It is not quite that systematic when you have a house full of kids all doing their own thing.

As I reflect on my experiences and offer advice and encouragement to new mothers or those women about to take that huge step in expanding the family, I don't want you to think I was perfect at this. There were times where I realized that I was missing the mark as a wife. In the next chapter you will see that even though Raman and I mindfully worked together to make everything possible in our home and careers, you can still get so caught up in events that you lose track of what you hold dear.

CHAPTER 7

Molding a family is worth all the effort you put into it.

One thing you must guard against is getting so caught up with the children that you forget about your partner. The reality is that there are only 24 hours in a day and the more people you have competing for your attention, the odds are good someone is going to suffer if you aren't careful. I loved being a mom, wife, and doctor. I tried my best to give the time each of those titles deserved, but we all need a reality check once in a while.

Mine came as I was planning Arya's first birthday. The first celebration is such a milestone for both the child and parents. You all survived your first year. Depending on the child, he or she is much more active. This is where the baby is walking or about to do so. The child is also learning how to communicate and is a unique little person at one year old. It is a great time to throw a celebration.

At this point, I had two kids, I was actively pursuing my medical career, and I was planning a birthday party. Several times in the month leading up to the party, Raman came to me and asked to talk. I kept putting him off. After all, it couldn't be that important, and I was juggling more balls than anyone should be allowed to do at one time.

Finally, two days before the party, I was at the kitchen table going over some last-minute details. Raman came into the room and said, "Sheenu, we have to talk."

I looked up in exasperation. "Dear, can't this wait until after the party? I have a ton of things I still have to do."

He sat down across from me. He reached out and gently but firmly took my hand, lifted the pen I was holding, and put it down on the table. He looked me right in the eyes and said, "No. I have been trying to talk to you for three weeks, and I am going to explode if we don't talk now."

This situation was different. Raman rarely started any conversation with this type of gravity in his voice. I had a slight sickening feeling in my stomach. I sat up straight in my chair. Trying to keep any fear out of my voice, I asked, "What's wrong?"

He gave me a little smile and said, "You know we haven't been spending a lot of time together." As I started to object, he held up both hands. "I know, I know," he quickly continued. "We have two little ones around, and we are both going crazy at our offices. There isn't enough time in the day to do everything. I am apprehensive that it is affecting our marriage." He took a deep breath and said, "Something happened to me a few weeks ago that made me realize we have to do something different."

I wasn't sure where he was going, and I didn't like the tone of his voice. I quietly said, "Go on."

"There was a female colleague at the hospital who kept approaching me. At first, it was about medical situations she was dealing with concerning some of her patients. About a month ago, her attention became stronger, and the conversations began to be more of a personal nature. It dawned on me one day that she was looking for more than a professional relationship between the two of us."

As the words settled in, the sickening feeling in my stomach started to roar to full-blown nausea. I thought I was going to throw up. All I could manage was to squeak out the word, "And?"

Raman reached over, took one of my hands, and held it between his two. He softly said, "Absolutely nothing happened. I politely told her that I kept my time with colleagues strictly professional, and she was smart enough to get the hint. However, warning bells started ringing very loud in my head. I don't ever want to get us in a position where either of us is tempted by someone else because we don't spend time together anymore. I mean," he gave a crooked grin, "look how long it took me to get your attention so that we could have this talk."

I started to ask what he meant, and I thought back to the past couple of weeks when he wanted to talk, and I brushed him off. For a moment, I felt like the worst wife in the world. I fought back the tears. From when we had first started going together, we had always been close. We did so much together. I loved our growing family. Sometimes we need a cold dose of reality to put life into perspective. We were around each other a lot dealing with the children and running to work, but we had lost that emotional intimacy that we always had.

The other realization hit me as I thought, "I'm not Superwoman. I can't do it all!"

Most of the time, the "awareness" portion of the 5 A's is reasonably self-evident. You know there is a problem. Then there are times like this where it smacks you in the face because you didn't see it coming.

Raman and I talked a great deal that night. It was nice to connect with my husband and my best friend like that again. We figured out that it was okay to acknowledge our limitations and that what we were trying to do with our careers and our family was too much. The answer was to get help with the children. We soon brought in an au pair. An au pair is live-in help who works for the family to help with the children.

It was a rather simple solution to a complex problem. There were some issues we learned to address with someone new living at the house, but we navigated them pretty quickly. Soon we fell into a new routine that was a little less hectic than our old one. Raman and I had time again for each other, and we treated ourselves to some alone time and doing things we used to do before kids. We went out to dinner, explored the city, and made time together to spend with friends. Sometimes as parents, you become so involved with the business of raising kids and trying to balance careers with a personal life, that it is easy to forget about yourself and your partner. A couple has to be vigilant against any situations that can take happiness away. A good relationship doesn't merely happen; both parties have to work at it consistently.

Having the au pair certainly made having our third child a little easier than the first two. It was still great and crazy and stressful at times, but I didn't have to worry about the other two so much. As a parent, you can never forget about the emotional needs of the children when you are bringing another little one into the house. Sibling rivalry can start young, and you want the kids you have to love their new brother or sister. Only the mom and dad can effectively take away any fears a child might have that they will be loved less when the new child enters the scene. For me, though, the au pair took away the constant worry about the other children — getting dressed, being fed, getting to play dates or certain appointments — practical matters like that. Having that extra help took a massive weight off my shoulder.

Time is such a valuable commodity. You can have unlimited love for your family, but that is constrained to 1,440 minutes a day. Unless physicists bust the space-time continuum, we are stuck with what we get each day. I believe one of the hardest things a person does is try to maximize their use of time. No matter what you do, there never seems to be enough of it. When you have a child, the problem is magnified. Have three children, and you can't even figure out the math!

Weaved into finding enough time for everything was that Raman and I wanted to bring our Indian heritage into our children's lives. Here is where I applied my 5 A's. I wanted my children to know and be proud of their heritage as they grew up to be young Americans. All families want to do this in some way with their respective culture, but it is different when you are alone in a country. Having grown up with a family connection where you see grandparents, aunts, uncles, and cousins all the time, I felt like the children would miss out on this crucial part of their life if I did not figure out how to provide the same opportunities under different circumstances. I knew we would not be like other families I knew in New York who seemed to always have a big Sunday dinner every week with many family members. All the same, I was determined to have the children learn and appreciate their heritage.

The extended family we built up in America through friends and colleagues was terrific, and many events in my children's lives were full of people, including family if we were visiting India or relatives were over here. I believe the important way to approach not having a great deal of family around is to mindfully make the best out of the situation. Technology makes regular communication easier now, even more so than when my children were young. Skype, social media, and inexpensive phone calling simplifies communication and enables it to be frequent. You set up a laptop and your family a half world away can be "at" your child's first birthday party!

We brought our culture into all aspects of family life starting when the children were young. Raman and I thought life was hectic when the kids were toddlers and in grammar school. Their demands on our time seemed to increase exponentially when they entered middle school and high school. They had unlimited interests it seemed. They were all excellent athletes and played various sports. They were in different clubs and doing things with friends. It was not easy to keep track of who was doing what. We had a big calendar where we tried to post everyone's activities. When the kids had the responsibility of keeping their activities up-to-date on the calendar and forgot to put something on there, the child who didn't post their activity had the lowest priority of getting a ride to where he or she had to be. This habit taught them to keep the calendar updated!

The craziness we went through was not any different than other families. I believe it helped teach all of us lessons. Number one is not to lose track of the idea that everything done in the family is with love. Nobody, not even the mother and father, is going to get to do everything they want. When you have to tell someone that it is not possible to do something because of time, schedules, or money, there is going to be disappointment. Raman and I tried to get very good at making sure whatever child we had to say "no" to knew that it did not mean we loved them any less.

This does two things. One, it helps prevent parents from spoiling a child. Second, it shows everyone how to look for compromises or alternative solutions. Sometimes there aren't any, but it teaches a child to look outside their narrow scope of what they want to do. I say child, but this is something we dealt with during the teen years more than any other time. I guess as humans, we would all like to have our way, but realizing early on that is not always going to happen is a good life lesson. Figuring out a different way to do something is an invaluable life skill your child will use forever.

Communication is another skill we steadily worked on and developed within the family. Raman and I were always very good at that, but apparently, we even needed a wake-up call at times. I am not sure what it is like when you only have one child. You are going to need communication between the child and parents, but several children make the communication factor an even higher priority. I believe my children had a good handle on how to talk with others with all the practice they had in the home. One thing that I am sure of is that they speak to others better than they spoke to each other at times! However, they sometimes learned the hard way that if they did not effectively communicate their idea or what they wanted to others, the boys were going to be on the outside looking in.

One other lesson my children learned growing up in our home is the importance of scheduling. I am not even talking about the calendar with their activities on it. What I mean here is how to allocate their time for what they wanted to do. Between sports, their lessons, and all the other activities, all three of them needed to develop a certain amount of self-discipline to be successful at what they wanted to do. Did they procrastinate on certain things, especially school papers and projects? Of course, they did! However, they did learn the dangers of procrastination when balanced against everything else they wanted to do. It isn't a bad thing for children to learn early on that a person has to schedule their time wisely.

As a parent, you love your children, and you enjoy having them around (most of the time), but your big responsibility as a parent is to develop your brood to leave the nest eventually. You want them as prepared as possible to minimize the difficulties that they will face once they leave your care. One of the hardest things we face as parents is knowing that it is impossible to be there for everything that they are going to face. The next best thing we can do is have them as prepared as possible.

In a two-parent household, it is imperative that both partners are on the same page when it comes to raising children. By having a unified front regarding rules, consequences, expectations, etc., children will know where they stand and how the family operates. This is for two reasons. The first reason is for the sake of the children. A child functions better when the family boundaries are apparent. It is difficult for anyone, let alone a young person, to operate in an atmosphere of ambiguity.

The second reason is for the sake of the parents. A child can detect a weakness faster than any two opponents facing off in a competition. If they see one parent is going to be easier to deal with regarding specific situations, then that is the parent they will go to. This ends up putting a great deal of pressure on the one parent and raises the potential for conflict with his or her partner. This talent is not something a child learns; they seemed to be born with it!

The years we raised the children went too quickly. It might not always seem so at the time, but now I think it passed at hyperspeed. Our situation wasn't that much different than any other family. However, we did have the extra component of bringing our heritage from India into our home to our children. They embraced it, and I believe they are better off for having done so.

CHAPTER 8

Having more than one child has its unique challenges.

Raising three boys is hectic at the best of times. When the two older ones were in high school and it seemed like everyone in the house was busier than ever, I had an auto accident. The crash was pretty bad, and I ended up with severe neck and lower back problems. As a doctor, I have certainly seen patients lament their lack of health and mobility. I have sympathized with them, but now I was in complete empathy with their plight. I was in pain and it was difficult to do almost anything for quite a while.

That didn't stop things happening in our home though. With five people who were active in work, school, and activities, there was rarely a calm moment. I mentioned before that as the boys were growing up, Raman and I introduced them to their Indian heritage. Our house became an eclectic mix of Indian and American customs. I want to share with you a bit about our holidays.

One of the boys' favorite Indian holiday is Diwali, which means "row of lights" in Sanskrit. It is the Hindu festival celebrating the triumph of light over darkness and good over evil. In a country of many holidays, it is a national holiday in India and the biggest festival of the year. Diwali falls somewhere in October or November, depending on the lunar calendar. I remember how Avi and Arya loved to share this holiday with the kids in their class in school and would take sweets in to give out to their classmates. It was a fun time in our home and a time that we all looked forward to a great deal.

Then there was the year that our sons came to us and said they wanted a Christmas tree! Thus started another tradition in our home that we all ended up embracing. We started out with the annual tradition of choosing a tree and doing all the Christmas activities. We would see the tree lit up at Rockefeller Center in New York City and go to Radio City Music Hall to see the Rockettes, the annual Christmas show. We would listen to the traditional Christmas carols played in St. Patrick's Cathedral. There was Christmas music in the house, gift giving, and pretty much everything involved with the holiday.

Looking back, my sons had the best of both worlds! There is certainly nothing wrong with that. We were doing what immigrants had been doing for the last couple of centuries. We celebrated our culture while embracing our new country. To be clear, America was only new to Raman and me. It wasn't something that I ever gave persistent thought to, but sometimes it hit me that my sons were Americans. I can't say that it ever occurred to me growing up that any children I had wouldn't be citizens of India. I looked at people I worked with and saw many men and women who had done the same thing. Nobody was sorry their children were born in a country different than their native one, but that didn't mean the parents weren't proud of their culture and worked so that their children also embraced their heritage.

It was always a happy marriage of traditions and cultures in our house — for the most part. Our food choices at home were an issue at times. I was a vegetarian since I can remember. That was how my parents raised me, and I kept up my diet when I moved to the United States. Raman was that way too, but he started to adapt to a more American diet. My sons were all into the foods of their friends, and this started to become a point of contention at home. When our parents and other relatives came to visit from India, I made sure everything at home was strictly vegetarian.

This issue shows the power of compromise. It wasn't always easy to get there, but we finally came up with a policy of vegetarian at home, and the children could eat anything outside of the house. One thing I learned over the years is that there are going to be bumps in any family. Some are going to be speed bumps while others will seem to be the size of Mount Everest. You can take solace that mountaineers surmounted even Everest eventually. Trying to incorporate different cultural preferences into a house can add conflict to the family dynamic. Dealing with something as routine as what food I served is a perfect example. It isn't a trivial matter as eating is necessary and enjoyable. It took a little trial and error to reach our dietary compromise and for all to embrace it, but I believe it is a good illustration how our family worked together and interweaved our different cultures and beliefs.

One thing Raman and I never lost our passion for was travel and discovering new places. Now we included our children in our adventures. We always tried to have vacation and travel opportunities as a family. I know too many families who do not make an effort to go away together. I greatly encourage it. Even on a budget, you can make local trips.

The point is not so much the where, but having the entire family together. Let's face the facts of life. Raman and I were not much different than many families. We both worked, and our children were incredibly active. It wasn't too long before everyone gathering around the table for a meal was more of a novelty than the norm. A vacation has the family together in a way that you aren't at home. You travel together, eat together, go to activities or attractions together, and become closer as a family. You get to know each other again. The parents are more relaxed because they left work behind for a week or two and children do not have friends or activities as a distraction.

We relished these opportunities to be together as a family. Some trips were within a day's drive of New York City while others were all over the country or international. There were times our vacation meant going to visit relatives in India. It was a terrific opportunity to have the boys spend time with grandparents and other family members. It helped them to connect the dots in their mind about their heritage and where it originated. It certainly reinforced everything they were learning from us.

The rest of what I dealt with raising three boys has nothing to do with what country you are from or your culture. I think there is a universal dynamic that affects families whether you live in Oshkosh, Wisconsin, or a village in Nepal. The dynamic can change with the number of children you have and if both parents are present, but there are common issues we all face when we have children.

To fully paint the picture for you, Avi and Arya were born within a couple of years of each other. Aru came into the world ten years after Arya. I had two boys close in age, and the other was not part of their world. While Aru was growing up, it was almost like he was a different generation than his older brothers. When he was starting school, Avi and Arya were active in high school.

The boys were outstanding in athletics since they were young. They loved sports and would play a variety of them as well as learn about them, read up on the ones they played, and watch them on TV. The two older boys had a group of friends from their teammates, and they did a lot of things together. Soon there were sleepovers with friends and even more activities as they expanded their social circle. As it happens with children, there would be some friends who would come and go, and then you would have the ones that were there from first grade until now.

When Avi and Arya were finding out they liked sports, and we started letting them play in local recreational leagues, I noticed that there weren't too many other Asians on their teams. At the time, there might not have been as many Asian families in the area we lived, or the kids didn't like sports. It could also have been a parental decision not to have them play. Now if I am driving past a soccer field or playground, it seems like you have representatives of many different countries and cultures playing together.

I remember thinking that my boys might get disconnected from their other friends of Indian or Asian heritage. They never let that happen. Maybe some of those friends didn't play sports, but Avi and Arya stayed linked with them through school and other activities. I think it dawned on me when the oldest was going to middle school that they were very proud of their Indian heritage. It was very much a part of them, and they were comfortable in who they were. Because of their connections through all their activities, they easily were able to talk, work with, and have fun with other kids of all backgrounds.

Sometimes as I listen to the news and the problems in the world, I realize that what my boys went through is happening more than ever with the diverse mix of people in America. It doesn't seem that children see much of a difference in race and heritage. They are very accepting of others and quickly mix with one another. If a parent, older sibling, or someone else doesn't give them ideas about how they are different, better, worse, or whatever, a child is not going to have much of a problem hanging around another child of an entirely different background.

When children are brought up around others who are different than they are, and work and play with them growing up, then they continue being able to relate to all kinds of people as they get older. I saw this in the two older boys as they started going through the higher grades and into college. Aru went through the same experiences as he followed behind his brothers a decade later in everything.

So, in Avi and Arya I had boys who were good athletes, students, and embraced their Indian heritage as well as their American background. They were incredibly active, and as I pointed out earlier, keeping up with everyone's schedule was a job in itself. One thing that I realize as a parent is that it all goes too fast. It is the usual cliché that you hear all the time when the kids are running you ragged, but it is true. When you are in the middle of a storm, you only want to make it out in one piece and on the other side of it. As parents, we sometimes get caught in that mind trap. However, when the boys get older and are not around so much, I look back on those times with fond nostalgia. I miss the crazy times. It is most likely because they are not around you every minute and you miss them!

Having two brothers who were close together in age was challenging. They loved each other. I do not doubt in my mind that if a bully were threatening one brother, then his brother would back him up and help him. It wouldn't matter which one was in trouble; the other one would be there for him. The problem was that five minutes after one saved the other, they would be ribbing each other and being playful.

Sibling comparison was prevalent in school and among their friends and social circles. I think there should be a mathematical formula showing that the closer in age the siblings are, the worse the comparison, especially if the older one is more mature for his age. I guess what it comes down to is that everyone has a need to be noticed and recognized for who they are. For most children, the first ones they want this validation from is their parents. Any child might think that this is difficult to achieve if they are the only one in the house. It is even more difficult when that child has a sibling in age proximity. Then it becomes a mathematical equation of comparison. It doesn't seem that children ever grasp the concept that parents love all their children.

Avi and Arya were no strangers to the comparison equation. Avi used to love taking care of his younger brother at home and school. Arya was also cool with his brother looking out for him. Avi focused on academic and athletic activities. While this was also important to Arya, he was much more social and liked to spend time with his friends. Also, Arya could be perky and inattentive at times in the classrooms. Teachers and fellow students compared the two brothers, telling Arya that he should be more focused at the school like his brother. This created a strain on the relationship between the two. Due to this comparison, the fun-loving and intelligent Arya experienced pressure to be somebody he was not.

Of course, this facet of their lives reached new heights when they became teenagers. The teenage years are when children begin to push for their individuality. They are on that discovery of who they are and what they want to do in life. All their peers are doing the same, and when you have someone at home doing the same thing, it heightens that awareness. They want that attention and validation from mom and dad in all they do.

My sons had a second obstacle when they were teens. They got a little brother!

Aru being born upset the applecart. They had no problem with the idea of a baby brother and welcomed him into our home with love and open arms. Then they found out how much work went into a baby. By that, I mean that there was something else to take the attention away from mom and dad. Of course, with a newborn, he gets an inverse amount of attention for his size. Once again, the joy and chaos of a baby filled our house. As his two older brothers found out, giving the baby so much attention didn't stop after only a year or so. We were on toddler and little boy duty while Avi and Arya started experiencing high school.

What Aru meant to them was dividing the parents' attention and time. The funny thing to remember in all of this was that this longing for the parents is unconsciously seeded. It is a human nature phenomenon. As I said before, it happens all over the world. For us, it meant a conflict between the two older boys.

For example, in academics, Avi was the type of student that school came easily. He could excel in most classes without much effort. All during high school, he was easily one of the best students in his entire class. Arya had to work harder at school than his brother. He was a good student, but it did not come as naturally. He did his best and did well at school.

It wasn't much different in athletics. They were both very good in sports. In high school, Avi became an excellent lacrosse player while Arya excelled at basketball. You would think that playing two very different sports would eliminate any comparison by the teachers and friends alike, but it didn't. The contrast became a source of annoyance between the two.

Then something happens that makes you realize that your children not only like each other but also love each other despite the distress between the two. The event took place at the conclusion of Avi's senior year. In fact, it was graduation day. The school had chosen Avi as valedictorian of his class. I wasn't kidding when I said he did well in school. Between his school work, activities, sports, etc., he achieved this high honor. Raman and I were so proud of him. Being valedictorian meant making a big speech at graduation and Avi worked hard at it.

Now during all the time leading up to his final act in high school, Avi was waiting to hear from Yale. He had been accepted in other schools but had not committed yet. Yale was his dream school, and he had not heard one way or the other from them. I took the other two boys to where the school was staging the graduation, and we settled into our seats. We saved a place for Raman as he was stopping home from his office and then meeting us there.

There are milestones in everyone's life. For a young person, high school graduation was the biggest. It was the door swinging from childhood to adulthood. It gives people a chance to reflect, and I felt like it was a milestone for me. With my oldest about to move on to college, it was a moment of change that I had to reflect on. I thought about how far I had come as a woman, wife, and mother since I came to the United States. It had been a tremendous journey, and I knew I still had far to go. I looked up at the stage where my oldest would be speaking and at the two boys around me. In moments like that you cannot but think that you had done something right.

Raman interrupted my stroll down memory lane when he took his seat next to me. He had a smile on his face and an envelope in his hand. I looked at the envelope and up at his face. It suddenly dawned on me why he had that look, and I said, "He got in?"

"Yes, he did. I wasn't even going to grab the mail on the way inside because I was running behind. When I did and saw the letter from Yale, I had to open it. I was almost afraid because I know how much this means to him. He is set to start in the fall!"

I think I did squeal with delight. I looked around, and I couldn't have been too loud as nobody was looking at us. Arya and Aru knew what this meant and were as excited as I was. I saw tears in Arya's eyes, and he asked, "When are you going to tell him?"

Raman answered, "When we go out to dinner after the graduation. We have reservations, and after we get seated and relaxed, I'll give him the news."

Arya looked at his father and asked, "May I give him the news?"

This request surprised both of us. We looked at each other and Raman raised a questioning eyebrow. I gave a slight nod, and he said to Arya, "Sure. I'll hold on to the envelope and slip it to you when it's time."

The ceremony started, and I sat back to watch. As the graduates approached their seats, I thought about what had gotten into Arya. After the last few years of their constant bickering and trying to one-up each other in almost everything, I realized just how much Arya loved his brother. Not only that, but he was also going to miss him a great deal! I glanced over, and Arya was working hard to keep up a brave face. This milestone hit him too. His brother was going off to college and starting a new phase of his life.

The rest of the ceremony was a bit of a blur. There were music and speeches. Avi's valedictory speech was excellent, and the audience gave him warm applause. I might have had a tear in my eye listening to his speech and when he received his diploma. It was everything graduation should be.

We waited for a while afterward as Avi hugged his friends and teachers after the ceremony. Finally, we left and headed to the restaurant. Avi was thrilled and chatty on the ride. Graduation had been an almost perfect punctuation mark on his high school career. Now that it was done, including his speech, he looked like the weight of the world was off his shoulders.

Sitting down for dinner was a relief for the entire family. There was a lot of laughter and joy around the table. After the server took our order, I saw a slight movement between Raman and Arya. My second oldest took a deep breath and loudly cleared his throat to get everyone's attention. When we were quiet, Arya said to Avi, "We might have had our differences while we were growing up, and maybe a lot worse at times." We all laughed. "I have to tell you, though, that I am proud to call you my big brother."

Arya continued, "I do have a special letter here to read." He pulled out the paper, and I noticed he kept it close to him so Avi couldn't see the Yale letterhead. Taking another deep breath, he read, "Dear Avi, it is with great pleasure that we inform you of your acceptance to Yale University beginning in the fall."

Avi looked surprised as Arya finished the short letter. Almost tentatively, he asked, "This isn't a joke?"

Arya answered, "No, big bro, it's real. You're going to Yale, bro!"

With that, Avi jumped up and hugged his brother. Then he went around the table embracing the rest of his family. As he sat back down, I heard Avi say, "This day has been about as perfect as it could get."

I couldn't agree more.

CHAPTER 9

It is good to be open to whatever life brings you.

There are many gratifying moments in a mother's life. We watch our children grow through milestones. I think all parents celebrate when their child smiles for the first time, starts to crawl, and then takes that first tentative step. We all remember when they begin talking, and sometimes wonder as they get older if they will ever stop! Soon, it is the first day of school, and you embrace their success in the classroom, their athletic endeavors, and any other activity or interest that they take up. It seems like before you know it they graduate high school and it is off to college. With all the planning and work that goes into getting to college, those four years your child is in a university are probably the fastest four years of all! In the blink of an eye, they graduate and are getting on with their adult lives.

When you have more than one child, it is gratifying to see how they grow to love one another. As I mentioned in the last chapter, sibling competitiveness is always a big part of brothers and sisters. I saw it enough with my older two sons, but I had a friend's daughter tell me something interesting once. We were there for a family celebration that they were having, and this family has four children — two boys and two girls. I watched all four teasing and giving each other grief all evening. There was nothing malicious, but you could see the sibling conflict at times. Later that night, the one daughter was talking about how she had to defend her younger brother at school.

I asked, "You guys have been going at each other all night. But you still stick up for each other?"

She said, "We do that amongst ourselves all the time. However, we are the only ones allowed to do that. Anyone else has to get through the rest of us."

I thought that captured the attitude of siblings beautifully. It certainly helped describe the brotherly relationship between Avi and Arya. When Avi went off to his first year at Yale, Arya seemed like a fish out of water. He missed his brother. When you are so close in age and have been together for 16 years, it is hard to be apart. Raman and I missed Avi too, and it was a different atmosphere around the house. Slightly less hectic and a bit quieter, but you could feel Avi's absence. I believe Arya felt this even more than we did.

Avi had sailed through high school, as his being chosen valedictorian attests. Arya was a good student too, but he had to work harder at it. When Avi left, Arya seemed to take it upon himself that he had to be as good in school as his brother was. This came strictly from him as neither Raman nor me put any extra pressure on him at all. Sometimes, self-inflicted pressure is the worst of all because you can't get away from it. At this point, Arya was a junior, and all of us were starting to look at colleges and the admission process as we did with Avi two years earlier.

Avi called us a great deal, and I am sure I mentioned some of the difficulties his brother was having. As for his first year of college, Avi had done well and was excited about taking part in a study abroad program he had been accepted into at Yale. He was going to Europe, and I was happy for him, even though I was a little apprehensive. After all, it was less than a year ago he left for college, and now he was headed to Europe. I was confident that he would do well overseas and would be fine, but mothers can always worry about their children.

One evening after we knew about the study abroad program, Avi called me and said, "I have an idea. Why don't you send Arya over to Europe with me during the summer? I get a break for a few weeks, and he can join me. We'll have fun, and maybe I can help Arya feel a bit more settled before he goes into his senior year."

I told him that I would talk to his father about the idea and get back to him. Part of me instantly thought that it was a great idea. If Arya went to Europe, he would have a chance to be with his brother and help their relationship grow more. If he didn't, he wouldn't see Avi at all on his summer break. Avi could do a great deal for his brother to calm him down and get him ready for his last year of high school. I also never thought travel was a bad idea as my children seemed to have a love for travel in their DNA as their mother and father did!

The other part of me had some motherly and practical worries. It seemed to be a little frightening to send my 17-year-old off across the ocean for a month or so. Plus, we did have some tentative plans to do college visits and other things related to getting Arya ready for his senior year in high school. Raman and I did discuss the idea with Arya, and in the end, we all agreed it was a good idea. Arya was off to Europe with his brother!

While I did have my fears, the trip went very well for both brothers. I don't think I could sum up how it went any better than the following email from Avi. It pretty much covered all the worries and expectations I had for the trip.

Hello all,

I am writing this from a little hotel room we are sharing in Paris. It is slightly bigger than the family car, but if we stick our heads out the window and stretch to look past the corner of the building next to us, we can see the top of the Eiffel Tower. Nothing but the best here for your sons!

Seriously, we are having a good time since we arrived here three days ago. We have walked the streets and have had some wonderful meals at little cafes that dot the streets. We did go to the top of the Eiffel Tower because that is what one is supposed to do in Paris. It was fun, and we can now say we did it. Yesterday, we spent almost the entire day at the Louvre. I thought the Metropolitan Museum of Art was big, but the Louvre is even more immense. We were there all day and didn't even take a break for lunch, but we still had areas we never got to. We saw the Mona Lisa. This might be sacrilege to art aficionados, but I didn't see the big deal. It was a lot smaller than I thought it would be and we waited in line for a while to see it. I hope Leonardo da Vinci forgives me.

Arya and I have had some good conversations. We covered a little of everything — school, sports, girls, family, the past, the future, the big deal with the Mona Lisa, and so much else. Don't worry about the girl conversation; I didn't say anything to lead him the wrong way! Ha ha!

This is our third week together, and I have seen a change in Arya. He is more at ease and smiling a lot compared to when he landed. I think it took almost a week for him to relax. I don't mean in terms of him hanging with me. I think we felt like we were back in the kitchen at home teasing each other within five minutes of meeting at the airport. That wasn't the problem. To me, he was wound tighter than he can usually get. I know he would be like that before a big test or a big game he was playing in, but it would leave him as soon as the event was over. This must be what you were telling me about on the phone with how he was handling this past school year.

If nothing else, I reminded him that it was okay to have fun, even with all he was trying to do. I know our personalities are different, but I told him he would turn into an old man before his time if he kept stressing about every little thing. I told him that high school and college were more like a marathon than a sprint. You have to pace yourself to accomplish what you want and enjoy the journey while doing it.

I think the act of a real journey this summer is helping him see that. Things have been going fairly well though we have hit a few speed bumps. We missed a couple of buses and trains in our travels, and one time we got on the wrong train. I did explain that to Dad when he asked me about the credit card charges in Switzerland when we were supposed to be in Austria. Oops!

Four days ago, we were in Barcelona where we had a much too real bonding moment. And before you have a heart attack, Mom, everything came out well. We were leaving a charming restaurant that was owned by an Indian couple who moved to Spain twenty years ago. We told them about our life in America and how you two moved there years ago. They were so nice and treated us to dessert. They even gave us some drinks to go in takeout cups.

I digress. When we left and headed back to our hotel in town, we felt like we were being followed. When we turned, we had two guys come up to us. They might have been our age but seemed older and were heavier. As they stopped about four feet away from us, one of them showed us a big knife that we could clearly see under the streetlight. Barely speaking English, they asked us for our money. All our time living in the New York City area, and we had to come all the way to Spain to be mugged.

Arya moved closer to me, and I could feel him start to tremble. I had a knot in my stomach. As they got a little closer, I loosened the lid on my cup. I said to Arya, "Do you know how you always said you could beat me in a race?" He just looked at me as if I was crazy. I told him, "Now you can try to prove it." With that I threw the rest of my drink in the face of the dude with the knife, shouted, "Run!" and we took off. We easily outdistanced them, and as we ran around a corner and into the street, we almost ran right into the side of a police car.

Fortunately, the officer behind the wheel spoke pretty good English, and we told him what just happened. He spoke into a radio, and he and his partner took off. Another police car screeched to a stop near us in about 30 seconds, and that officer told us to wait. Soon there were cops all around. I think Arya was scared, but he looked at everything as if he was a tourist in Times Square. The short version of what happened is that the cops we first ran into caught the two. They were still jogging towards where we went, so they were easy to nail. Apparently, these two had been terrorizing the area, especially tourists, for a couple of weeks. There were so many cops in the area because they were trying to find the two. We did go to the police station for about an hour to file a report, and the police drove us back to the hotel. They said there was a chance we might be asked to come back to testify, but they already had so much on the two that probably would not be necessary.

I think it all hit both of us as we got back to our room. We both started shaking and held each other. There was a mixture of laughing and crying going on, and we were both guilty of it. I think Arya and I have never felt closer than we have the past few days since then.

That's our adventures so far. We are doing well, and the thing in Spain was just being in the wrong place at the wrong time. For the most part, the people have been great wherever we go, and we are having the time of our life. I will make sure that Arya returns to you in one piece.

I love and miss all of you. Give Aru a hug from us.

Love, Avi

PS – Thank our high school coaches for getting us into such good shape!

Arya did get home in one piece, and it was a marvelous experience for both brothers. I think they found out that you can be physically apart but still close. Arya was a little calmer going into his senior year. He still had some anxiety and worked a little too hard at times, but I believe the trip did him a world of good.

As for me, my career was progressing nicely. I moved into an administrative position where I was managing a large team of people. An observation I made long ago is that when you unselfishly give yourself in helping those under you, then everyone's career seems to move forward. After all, working for others to achieve their success is naturally going to make the manager a success.

I didn't only concentrate on work where my people were concerned. Since I came to the United States, I had many colleagues help me with almost every aspect of my life. Many in my past showed me the ropes in school, how the medical profession worked in this country, how to cope with having a career and family, etc. This extended to the best places to shop or what restaurants were worth going to for dinner.

As the saying goes, I was determined to take all that others had done for me and "pay it forward." I made sure that I was there for anyone who needed help, including the recent arrivals from other countries. I knew what it was like to be "a stranger in a strange land" away from family.

One person I remember vividly, I will call Sue. She was one of my junior colleagues and wrestling with a common issue among women — how to maintain a successful professional and family life at the same time. She was from an Asian country whose traditions had the wife and mother putting everyone else's welfare before hers. She didn't come to me for help, but I could see that she was having some problems in the performance of her professional duties. One day, I asked her what was wrong, and it was like I opened a dam. The poor woman had been keeping so much inside and needed a friendly ear to unload on. And unload she did!

When she finished, I started to share with her some of what I had gone through and discovered during my career as a doctor, wife, and mother. We continued this conversation over the course of months. Slowly, she started to improve her performance at work, and she said things were slowly getting better at home. Her journey reminded me that while we would love the difficult things in life to change at the snap of the fingers, it usually occurred in increments.

At one point I shared with Sue my 5 A's of Awareness, Assess, Adapt, Adopt, and Act. I noticed that she was a good student when she was dealing with a problem at work. I happened to glance at a notepad in her hand one day, and she had the issue she was dealing with listed at the top of the page with the 5 A's under it. She had some notes next to the first few A's as she was proceeding through the steps. I asked her about it, and she said that she had adopted it for almost every problem she encountered now. Sue first utilized the system at home when she was trying to figure out a dinnertime that met everyone's schedule.

Working with Sue in this way was a revelation to me. I enjoyed being a help and coaching her to a better performance. Her happiness with the positive direction her life was going made me feel good too. I also found out that by reviewing how I approached problems and made decisions, I was reinforcing the concept in my mind. For whatever reason — laziness, too much on our brain, distractions — we don't always stick with something that works for us. It is an act of mindfulness to stay with a good practice. My working with others on the 5 A's allowed me to return to it for my own decision-making more frequently than I might have done otherwise.

This experience made me realize that there was something for me to do if I became weary of being a full-time doctor. I knew I would want to find something where I was still helping people. I am certainly wired to help others, which was one of my motivations for entering the medical field in the first place. I think it was then that I entertained the idea of becoming a coach to others, especially women who were struggling with finding that sweet spot where career and personal life intersect when everything is going well.

It was also the first time a book on the subject, especially coming from an immigrant in America, popped into my mind. I liked the concept, and it was in the back of my mind for several years before I brought it to fruition. I do look at becoming this type of coach as the next phase of a very full, productive, and happy life.

CHAPTER 10

The journey is always ongoing as we look for new ways to help others.

When I think of the different phases of my family, I marvel at the journey and the different directions it takes. I often get excited about where it is going to go next. When I think of watching Avi and Arya grow up and go through high school, college, and embarking on their lives as young adults, I am in awe of how well they did. I hope their little brother, Aru, will follow in their path. Raman and I learned a great deal about ourselves as a couple and as parents with the first two. Hopefully, Aru will be the beneficiary of that hard-won knowledge. Of course, with each child is an opportunity to discover new challenges!

To finish up on my reminiscing about Avi and Arya, I want to share that Arya made it through the rest of high school just fine. The trip to Europe with his brother did wonders for him. While Arya still tended to stress over important events in his life, he learned to achieve balance. He received an athletic scholarship to attend engineering college and went through that experience with flying colors. Avi trained to be a lawyer. It is gratifying to see your child embark on his chosen profession with enthusiasm and commitment.

While the older boys went through college and started on their careers, something started to happen that I wasn't quite prepared for. They started dating! I think as a parent that I knew it was going to happen but never thought about it much until it began. When you love your children and enjoy having them around, it is difficult to remember that the goal of parenting is to prepare the children to be out on their own!

There were many times in high school and college where both boys went out as a group with all their friends. Determining if any one person in the group was "dating" another was usually a mystery, at least to me. However, it was not a bad way to be socially active with both genders without any issues having to do with commitment or jealousy or any of that type of thing. They were young people having fun and learning how to relate socially. If I asked if the girl they were going to the movies with was their "girlfriend," the inevitable reply was, "Yes, she's a girl, and she is my friend." This was different from my growing up years. While I remember meeting Raman and us starting a courtship that led to marriage, I do not recall doing much casual dating. You went out with someone because you liked them and hoped it would turn into something permanent.

I realized the times had changed. This isn't necessarily a bad thing.

Avi and Arya helped make me realize that casual dating was fun and didn't necessarily mean that the girl that they were going out with was going to be the "one." I believe they were both open to that happening. They just weren't rushing it.

I noticed that was true with all their friends. In fact, between their social groups and what I saw at work, men and women wait a great deal longer to get married than young people did when I was their age. I wouldn't change my life, but I can see where that isn't for everyone. I have seen people date for years before getting married and waiting longer to have children. One young couple

I know in their 30s dated for seven years before getting married. Now after five years of marriage, they are having their first child. She will be 35, and he will be 33 when the baby is born. You can tell they are very happy together and they approached their life with a degree of maturity that would have been lacking if they married within a year of first meeting.

The other thing I noticed with my children and those of my friends is that young people today are so accepting of other races and beliefs. It is not unusual for my sons to be in a group of friends from different countries and different backgrounds as well as Americans whose family has been here for five generations.

I am a firm believer that the younger generation can learn much from their elders. However, I also believe that older men and women can learn just as much from the young ones.

What I started to notice as time went on is how people from different backgrounds started to mingle. While many people honored their heritage, it didn't mean they couldn't find happiness with someone from a different race or belief system. Would there be conflicts? Of course, there would be, but there are in every relationship, even if you grew up in the same town three houses over from your future mate. If Arya comes home with a lovely girl of Italian heritage, it only makes our family richer by the association.

My career gave me ample opportunities to see how all these people from different countries and cultures could work together and enjoy each other's company. As the older boys were going through college, I found myself managing units in three different sites simultaneously. I know by working in New York City that I am going to have a variety of personalities and heritages on my staff. It helped reinforce for me that people are all the same. The vast majority of people want to give their best at their job, get along with their colleagues, and be proud of the work they do.

Now, as an administrator, I had to help facilitate all that even if I didn't speak the same language as they did, understand their customs, or they learned different ways to do things at work. There are two ways to handle a situation like this. You can yell and scream to make everyone conform to your way. The alternative approach was to coach people, so they could comprehend why things were done in a prescribed manner and encourage them to reach a high proficiency in their duties.

The second way encouraged teamwork and veterans to help rookies work towards the common goals of the unit. It was also encouraged for new people to speak up if they thought they had a better way of doing something. You never know where a good idea is going to come from that would make everyone's life easier.

Managing multiple facilities was a great promotion and more responsibility. It coincided with having more freedom in my life. Aru was now in high school, and that opened up additional time in my life. Raman and I continued to do those things that we enjoyed together, and our family of five was a family of three very often. I found out that I had more time to spend and socialize with my colleagues and friends than I had ever done before.

The time I spent with them made me realize how many of the people I worked with were involved in interracial relationships or marriages. There were many Asians with Americans, and I was able to listen to some of their stories of how they merged their two backgrounds into their relationship. It made me think back to how our sons brought American traditions into our home, such as Christmas. I realized that I went through a lot of what my colleagues did by way of our boys rather than my spouse. Raman and I did a great deal of learning and adapting together as it was, so I could identify with much of what my colleagues shared with me.

It occurred to me that how I managed much of my life in a new country and raising three American boys was not a bad template for others to follow. Not so much the exact step-by-step process I went through since everyone's situation is different, but more about the attitude involved with bringing marriage and family together. I first looked at it in terms of different cultures coming together in a relationship but realized that the lessons I learned apply to relationships in general.

I sought out a business coach to help me firm up my ideas. She assisted me in putting together two clear concepts that shaped my life with my husband and my family. The first is that a happy relationship is the result of both halves of the couple working towards the same goals. The second is that each person, especially the woman, needs to know who they are. It is impossible to work towards goals if you do not know your strengths and weaknesses. I think many women have no problem identifying their weaknesses but are not as quick to know their strengths. A person needs to know themselves so that they know how to handle different situations as they arise.

Picture a tract of land that has some flowers and trees on it but has the potential to be so much more. Winding paths approach the land from different directions, and a man and a woman are heading towards it on separate paths. They eventually meet and decide that they can turn the area into a fantastic oasis. To do so, they need to find out what each can do and then bring their gifts to the mission at hand. There might be some setbacks, and things do not bloom as quickly as the couple would like, but if they keep at it, they soon have a flourishing oasis that is just about perfect.

In the back of my mind, I had been thinking about what I wanted to do if I made a career change. It wasn't something I would do tomorrow, but I don't think it is necessary for a person to do the same thing all their lives, no matter how good they are at it, if they feel a compulsion to do something else. There is no law preventing a change.

It was something I thought about at times. I had been working at my medical career before marriage and through all my adult life with Raman and raising our boys. I still had Aru, but after the first two, it would be easy working with him through school, sports, activities, and all those other milestones of youth.

I knew I still wanted to help people. That was always one of my driving forces in life. However, I realized it didn't have to be with the initials M.D. after my name. I realized that I had the insight to help people in different situations with my 5 A process. With it, I had success both in my personal life and my medical career. I was encouraged to further my relationship with the business coach. During our brainstorming, we decided to create retreats focusing on the theme of "Change your narrative, change your situation, change your future."

My business coach and I conducted retreats where I shared concepts based on my experiences. The purpose of these retreats was to help others resolve their problems. The emphasis was to use the 5 A process and help the women who attended to learn how to help themselves in any personal or professional situation they encountered. Let me share a couple of stories from those retreats.

One involved an Asian girl who was expecting her first child. She was very nervous because she had no idea how she was going to balance her work, new baby, husband, and finding any "me" time. As we talked, and Liu explained her situation to me, I saw myself in her. I lived what she was going through.

As I began to go through the 5 A's with her, Liu came to understand that by being aware and accessing her situation, her priorities had changed. I have discovered that part of what happens in life is that priorities are constantly shifting. Sometimes we get ourselves in trouble when we adamantly stick to our list of priorities without realizing that with the shifts in life, it is necessary to revamp the list. When we do that, then we can apply our focus in the correct areas of our life. The key is to deal with fears and come up with a workable plan to deal with them.

Liu was able to come up with different options for herself during the retreat, resolve her fears, and take action. As a soon-to-be mom, she had every new mother's anxiety. She wanted to be the best mom she could be as well as a good wife and to have continued success in her career. It was gratifying to see her come to the retreat with a complex issue and gain clarity.

To our surprise, she came back to our next retreat with her husband and baby. She shared with the whole group that after the first retreat, she went back and sat down with her husband and told him what she learned. Together, they put together a plan to maintain and grow their relationship. In the end, they determined to hire an au pair as well as have the grandparents visit when they were available. By enlisting the help of others, the husband and wife were able to maintain balance in all areas of their life.

At another retreat, a different kind of relationship conflict came to my attention that my coach and I were able to help. This time, the woman's name was Jenny, and she shared that she and her brother were very close to her father. Unfortunately, her dad had metastatic cancer, which means that cancer had spread enough that his chances of survival were very slim. He did not want to take palliative chemo. He only wanted to go home, be with his family, spend the rest of his days in prayer, and spend positive moments with his family.

As we explored the situation with Jenny, she broke down and cried. She said that she and her brother were hoping against hope that her father would live because they had lost their mom early in their lives. We applied the 5 A's to the circumstances and helped Jenny to realize that she had to let go of her desires and respect her father's wishes instead. She went home to take this perspective to her brother so that they all could spend quality time together as a family. The new goal was to give her dad great family time in his remaining days.

The results from our retreats fulfilled my heart with love and joy. I could see where I could find a fulfilling career doing this type of work. I continue to apply the 5 A process to this concept as I try to find the best path for me.

As my family gathered around the Thanksgiving table the following November, and we caught up with what was happening in our lives, I was truly thankful for my journey and where it brought me. I realized with confidence that I had other things to offer people, and I had already taken steps to make that dream become a reality. I plan to continue helping more people in the best way possible.

EPILOGUE

As the plane finally came into India for a landing, I smiled at my trip down memory lane and my dreams for the future. Flying had its frustrations, but nothing gave you more time to think than a long flight halfway across the world. When I released my seat belt and stood up ready to disembark, I felt a certain peace I had not felt for a while. I still was not completely sure what I was about to face concerning my mother, but I was ready for that. Furthermore, I knew that when I returned home, I was going to continue building my coaching business along with practicing medicine.

I did stay in India for a few weeks. My mother recovered, and I did a great deal of hand-holding with her and my father. Once I arrived in India, the memories I had on the flight over reverberated through my mind during the entire stay. They certainly helped me through some of the tougher days with my mother and father. It is hard watching as your parents get older and they learn to wrestle with their new reality.

While this would not be the way I would suggest doing it, the time away from home, family, and work gave me some time to think and reflect. I heartily endorse everyone to do that now and then, preferably not because of a sick parent. It seems that sometimes we need to physically get away from our day-to-day situation to think through life. In our increasingly busy lives, having quiet time seems extremely rare.

The time in India gave me some perspective on what I wanted to do in my professional life. My reflections emphasized how much I loved my husband and family. I do know I will embrace whoever my sons bring into their lives and mindfully work at them being a part of our family. I know that while they might not be all that serious in their dating today, either one of my older sons might meet somebody tomorrow that will turn their world upside down. As for Aru, I still have a few more years with him at home watching him grow. Then he will be off to college and whatever the future has in store for him.

On my way back to the U.S., I was very excited to come back home to be with Raman and the kids again. As I flew back in the other direction to return to the United States — my home — I thought in great detail about what I wanted in this book. If you can mentally write a book while spending 20 hours in the air, I did it. I imagined putting the words on paper would be a little more difficult, but it was a good start. The important thing is that I thought about how to tell my story to entertain readers and teach them some concepts that would be beneficial in life.

I flew into Raman's arms as I got out of the airport and I realized how much I had missed him. As we were driving back home, we caught up on things. We talked a great deal while I was in India, but it is not the same as being next to each other. After talking about my parents and his time here with our sons, I brought up the idea I had been kicking around in my mind. He encouraged me to think it through thoroughly and to discuss with my business coach. Raman has always been supportive of everything I do, and again, he did not disappoint me.

After resting for two days, I went back into my routine of living my life and being engrossed in practicing medicine. What was different is that I scheduled some additional time with my business coach. I told her I wanted to expand my coaching retreats. I explained to her about my opportunity to review and examine my life on my trip back and forth to India. I told her that I felt the next phase of my life was helping people as I always have, but differently than through medicine. We discussed what I wanted to do and explored the best way to go about it.

Through our talks, we figured out that my niche was reaching out to people — mainly woman, but men would be welcome — who were struggling in their search for a balanced life. Additionally, I could certainly offer valuable insight to immigrants who were separated from their families as they worked to establish themselves in America.

We thought my 5 A philosophy would make a solid foundation for all aspects of the type of coaching I would do with people. It was a formula that could be applied to any situation, just as I applied it to many personal and professional issues I faced in my life. Moreover, the 5 A's are invaluable when trying to find a happy balance between the personal and professional.

We also surmised that my years as a doctor would be invaluable for working with a client. When a person comes to a doctor with a malady, a good doctor appraises the situation, reviews all symptoms, and only then gives a diagnosis and treatment regime to the patient. It isn't any different when a person comes to you with a problem. You need to ask probing questions to figure out his or her real issues. Then you can help guide them to a possible solution.

I believe that my ultimate goal is to help people who are facing new situations in their life that are giving them trouble. What I help them do is bridge the new with the old, whether it is a generational gap, relationship gap, culture gap, or anything else that is an obstacle to living a joyous life. I want to support people through the different phases of their relationships with themselves and others. I know I can explain to others that they too can survive and thrive doing the same thing I did.

As I put the finishing touches on this book, my next step is working with other professionals to guide me through the next steps of my professional journey. I am excited about the idea of helping people in a manner that will be integral to their entire life. It is a little scary, but anything new usually is. I look forward to talking to you in the future about my new career and all the wonderful stories that result from it.

Will You Leave a Book Review?

Did you enjoy this book and find it useful?

We will be very grateful when you post a short review and give your success story right now!

Your support makes a difference. We read and respond to all the reviews personally to make this book even better!

www.ingramcontent.com/pod-product-compliance
Lightning Source LLC
Chambersburg PA
CBHW021155080526
44588CB00008B/357